T0147149

CATERING FOR MY KING

BARB VANVLEET

WESTBOW
PRESS®

A DIVISION OF THOMAS NELSON
& ZONDERVAN

This book is a work of non-fiction. Unless otherwise noted, the author and the publisher make no explicit guarantees as to the accuracy of the information contained in this book and in some cases, names of people and places have been altered to protect their privacy.

WestBow Press books may be ordered through booksellers or by contacting:

WestBow Press
A Division of Thomas Nelson & Zondervan
1663 Liberty Drive
Bloomington, IN 47403
www.westbowpress.com
844-714-3454

Because of the dynamic nature of the Internet, any web addresses or links contained in this book may have changed since publication and may no longer be valid. The views expressed in this work are solely those of the author and do not necessarily reflect the views of the publisher, and the publisher hereby disclaims any responsibility for them.

Any people depicted in stock imagery provided by Getty Images are models, and such images are being used for illustrative purposes only.
Certain stock imagery © Getty Images.

Scriptures taken from the Holy Bible, New International Version®, NIV®. Copyright © 1973, 1978, 1984, 2011 by Biblica, Inc.™ Used by permission of Zondervan. All rights reserved worldwide. www.zondervan.com The "NIV" and "New International Version" are trademarks registered in the United States Patent and Trademark Office by Biblica, Inc.®

ISBN: 978-1-6642-7935-3 (sc)
ISBN: 978-1-6642-7937-7 (hc)
ISBN: 978-1-6642-7936-0 (e)

Library of Congress Control Number: 2022917841

Print information available on the last page.

WestBow Press rev. date: 10/26/2022

To the One who healed and renewed my heart—Jesus Christ. And to Ed, who after forty years of marriage, is much more than a husband—he is my best friend. May we always take the high road, trusting Christ who goes before us.

Ed and I

CONTENTS

PART THREE

INTRODUCTION

HAVE YOU EVER OPENED AN orange and examined it closely? You would discover that each juicy section is made up of tiny pulps. Have you ever looked closely at a peanut shell and discovered that it is made up of hundreds of strong, dense fibers? Then breaking it open, you find a perfectly formed nut inside. Another amazing food is the onion. Peel away the paper-thin skin and cut it in half to expose layer after layer that form the onion bulb—that has an odor so strong it can burn your eyes and yet taste so good on a hamburger.

All my life I have been intrigued with the design of food. Like a flower with many parts, each part comes together to form its kind. Each time I peel a banana, cut into a kiwi, husk an ear of corn, or even gaze at the deep purple color of the plum, the intricate details intrigue me. In addition to each food's fascinating detail, there is unique, life-giving nutritional value in each one. It is easy for me to understand why I *need* the very fruits, vegetables, and grains God has created because they sustain my life. But I never understood my *need* for a Heavenly Father—until now.

The definition of need is a condition or situation in which something is required or wanted. Crops need water; people need affection; I needed a Savior to save me.

Before I was born, God already knew of my life's journey and the road I would travel. He knew of all the bumps that would set me off course, the peaks I would have to climb over, and the deep valleys I would have to climb out of. He also knew the times I would go the wrong direction and the turning points where that direction would be corrected. He knew of every obstacle that would be in my life and the things that would pierce my heart. *God knew all this, the end from the beginning;* He designed learning points and life lessons for the journey so that the "wrong" directions were never wrong but rather experiences so that I could grow and become the person He created me to be. However, all I knew was that I longed for healing from my past, peace that would give rest, joy that would spring from within, hope that would give assurance, and love that was unconditional! No person could give me all that—I needed a Savior.

Over time I began to understand God's ways. Just as in the Old Testament, when the people of Israel left God's path and He corrected them, He did so for me. Isaiah 30:21 says, "Whether you turn to the right or to the left, your ears will hear a voice behind you, saying, 'This is the way; walk in it.'"

Often God seemed to beckon me, saying, "I am here; don't give up!"

As I opened myself to my Heavenly Father along life's journey, I discovered that He revealed more of Himself and more of His plan to me. He set in motion the desire of my heart to combine my passion for food and my eagerness to serve. Then the day arrived when I placed my trust in Christ and began catering … for my King.

PART ONE

CHAPTER ONE

THE COUNTRY ROAD

I STOOD BY THE CAR, looking up in amazement at the small country school. My mother and younger brother, Rick, were almost to the steps. I thought, *How will all the kids fit inside that little school?*

It was the fall of 1965, and my family had just moved from a Minneapolis suburb out to the rural country town of Buffalo in Central Minnesota. We were exchanging city life for life in the country. Dad said, "It will be good for us."

So at the age of ten, there certainly were going to be many changes in my life and the lives of my two brothers as well. My elder brother, Steve, would take the school bus into town to attend high school, while my younger brother, Rick, and I would attend the one-room country school. One of those changes came the day our mother took us to see our "new" school, which was really quite old and was going to start in a week.

I ran to catch up to my mom and Rick as they stepped up onto the crumbling cement steps leading to the entrance of the little school. As a child, something small can appear big until we grow up. But even at the age of ten, I thought the building seemed small. Once inside the door, we were standing in a hall the length of the school. Coat hooks lined the wall, and there were doors at each end of the hall that we guessed led to classrooms.

While the teacher, with a reserved smile, introduced herself to our mother, Rick and I curiously peeked behind the door to the other side of the wall. To our surprise, or more like shock, there was only a small room with six short rows of wooden desks. Rick whispered to me, "This is weird."

The word *weird* did not describe it; the teacher told us she was the only teacher for all the grades, first through eighth!

Mom asked, "How many children are going to this school?"

We were amazed to hear the teacher say, "Thirteen."

Our amazement turned into disbelief when the teacher explained that the students oversaw all the chores. I quickly looked around, as my mind thought of making beds and washing dishes; those were the chores that I did. Immediately, the teacher, who now seemed annoyed, brought us over to a chart on the wall that plainly listed all the chores. On my tippy-toes, I stretched to read the list: clean the boys' and girls' outhouses, sweep the classroom floor but do not touch the mouse traps, carry water in from the outside well to fill the water fountain tank, and put books away in the library. Confused as to where a library might be, I turned around to find a five-foot-by-six-foot area with a small wooden table surrounded by old worn-out books. Suddenly, I started to miss my city school.

The first few days of school were an adjustment for us; the reality of change really hit after the fourth day. Unexpectedly, our mom and dad announced that we were going to start walking to school! We immediately protested, saying, "The school is at least twenty miles away!"

Thinking they had to be teasing, we soon found a lunch box and school bag placed in our arms, and to our disbelief, the back door opened up before us.

It did not take long before our new friends who lived down the country road from our house joined us in walking to school. The five of us, as if on an adventure, made our way through the field of alfalfa, crossing the pasture—while keeping a careful eye on the bull—over a hill, down to the lake, and then up the road to get to school. By the time we arrived, we had rocks in our pockets and wildflowers and sticks (swords) clutched in our hands. We looked as if we had been on a three-day wilderness trip.

We had adjusted to our country school by spring, although it was evident that our teacher had somewhat of a dislike for city kids. It was challenging, but Rick and I tolerated her favoritism toward the country kids.

Anticipation of summer vacation was growing, but that was not the only thing growing; Mom was expecting. It was a warm summer day in July, when my two brothers and I welcomed home our new baby sister, Nancy. With the addition, the rest of summer was busy.

The summer had flown by, and before we knew it, our lunch boxes and school bags were back in our hands as we headed out the back door for another year of school. Unknown to me at the time, it was during this next school year when I would face a realization that would affect me into my adult life.

Despite our attempts to be good, Rick and I had to accept the fact that we did not meet our teacher's country standards. Then one day my dislike for her grew even more when she literally hung Rick up by his shirt onto a coat hook out in the hall. He hung there with his shoes barely touching the floor for what seemed like hours. Whatever he had done to make her so mad I cannot remember, but I know it could not have been so bad because in a one-room classroom, you could see, hear, and know everything that went on. As a result, the teacher told my mother a story, but we knew differently.

Mom did not expose any unnecessary conflicts to our dad; therefore, he was oblivious to many situations. She would just say to us, "Kids, Dad doesn't need to know. He'll just get worked up."

The secrets meant peace of mind for her. Mom would listen or stand up for us, and Dad ... well, he would just say we "deserved it." The disagreement between them would always end up in a fight.

One day at school, I sat at my desk, fretting, while waiting for sixth-grade math to be called up. Math class always made me nervous, and I did not know why; I only knew I did not like it. Soon the teacher called the sixth-grade class up to the table in front of the classroom. There were only three of us: Carol, Jimmy, and me. On the blackboard, the teacher assigned a large-digit problem to each of us. Carol and Jimmy proudly gave their answers, getting it right. I sat focusing on the number, which seemed to jump around and mock me. I guessed, and the answer was wrong. Again, I guessed and was wrong. Soon the teacher demanded that I come up to the blackboard.

And as I guessed again, she moved me closer until my nose was touching the board. Suddenly, I could feel myself tremble and quickly was unable to hold back the tears. I could hear snickering and laughing behind me. Slowly, deliberately, I could feel the teacher's hands turning me around to face the class, who were all now silent in their seats.

The teacher said coldly, "This is what happens when you don't do your studies. You turn into a dummy!"

Humiliated, I quickly walked back to my desk, my head hanging and my chest heaving from crying. At that moment, the overwhelming realization hit me—I was not smart. I was dumb. Suddenly, my stomach hurt. It was really my heart, but I did not know it.

Late that spring, as school let out, I celebrated silently. This ended my last year in that school. I looked forward to going to high school along with my elder brother, Steve. But for now, it was summer vacation, and I was ready for it.

CHAPTER TWO

THE LAST SUMMER

IT WAS LATE IN THE summer, back before we moved from the city to the country, when Mom and Dad took Steve, Rick, and me along to look at an old farmhouse out in the country that was for sale. The owners greeted the family and then invited us to take a look around. We were checking out the upstairs when I said to my brother, "This house smells."

Suddenly, Dad's hand raised up, and his eyes pierced mine, and Mom knew not to say a word. I remained quiet for the rest of our time there.

When we arrived at another nearby farmhouse for sale to look it over, I knew to keep my comments to myself. And believe me, there was a lot I could have commented about. Eventually, this was the farm my parents bought.

There was not any running water in the house; therefore, it lacked a bathroom. It took some time to get used to the smelly little outhouse nestled in the trees by the shed. When it came time to take a bath, I yearned for the bathtub that was in our city house. Waiting for water to heat on the stove and then pouring it into a metal basin was not my idea of a bath.

Drinking and cooking water was drawn from an outside windmill pump. The kitchen sink had a pump handle that drew up water from the rain well—water that ran off the roof and into a cistern. Sometimes we would pump up debris and occasionally a dead frog or toad. Laundry was washed and put through an old wringer washer then hung outside to dry. But after the baby was born, Mom and I made many trips to town to wash laundry.

As Dad tried to renovate the old farmhouse, tension could be felt within its walls. It was decided that the house could not be salvaged and that we could not spend another winter in it. So Mom and Dad changed plans and decided to build a new house on the property. By that fall, with much excitement, we moved into the house, even though it was only roughed in.

Dad was a barber, and if he was not at the barbershop, he was working on the inside of the house, which meant we were working as well. Dad instilled good working habits in us, even though he tainted it by also instilling in us that we had to work or do something to meet his approval. We usually came up short, and he was more than happy to let us know it countless times. "Kids don't deserve anything unless they work for it," he would say. So work we did!

Despite Dad's impatience with us, he loved the farm and enjoyed the many opportunities it gave us. One day he surprised us with a pony and then two weeks later with a horse that was expecting! For the very first time, we got the privilege of watching a colt being born.

Every day there was something new to discover on the farm. One of my favorite enjoyments was to be in the garden that had been cultivated by the previous owners for years. In the spring, I'd get down on my hands and knees and plant seeds of all kinds. Fascination consumed me as the seeds grew and lush green plants filled the garden. But to my displeasure, other green plants were popping up as well. So with my baby sister usually by my side, I had the daunting task of perpetually pulling the weeds, a never-ending job! Before long, fruits and vegetables sprang up, and we celebrated and feasted on the garden's bounty.

I vividly remember picking raspberries off the bushes, holding each berry, examining the cluster of juicy droplets, then popping them into my mouth, savoring their sweetness. Sometimes Mom would have me pick peas for dinner. Pulling up the bottom of my shirt, I would gather pods and then carry them to a cool place to work. As I opened the pods, I became intrigued by each row of tiny green peas lined up perfectly like a row of soldiers. However, there was one garden crop that taught me the discipline of patience; that was watermelon. It seemed like an eternity waiting for the day that the first watermelon would be ripe for eating. Then one day Dad announced, "The watermelons are ready!"

The family would gather by the garden for the "big event." Dad would slowly cut into the first melon. Sounds of approval could be heard as seeds were spat in every direction. Not only did I enjoy my juicy, sweet slice for its incredible flavor, but also the fact that it came from our very own garden.

There was plenty to do around the farm. This summer Dad had us working on a project that no doubt changed us from the city kids we were to a breed of kids groomed to fit country life. Steve, Rick, and I had the tedious task of chopping down and clearing sumac and stinkweed by the lake, which was adjacent to the farm property. Our goal was to create a park-like setting for camping and picnics. Dad put Steve in charge of this project because he was the eldest. We began the project in all seriousness, but as days turned into weeks, the temptation to stop and goof around overcame us more and more often. However, we always had a listening ear for the sound of the "buggy," which meant our dad was coming!

The buggy was a car that had its roof, sides, and seats removed and wooden planks fastened to the floor. It was built for hauling tools and whatever else needed hauling. Often it was loaded with family and friends. Dad would take the people on a tour of the farm, showing off the projects being worked on. The engine was loud, which worked to our advantage because we could hear it coming down the path from a long way off. We would scurry back to work because the sound meant Dad was coming to check on our progress.

Steve was not only the leader of the work projects, but he also took leadership in our adventurous fun as well. One day, while working down by the lake, he decided that we would take a break. His plan was for Rick and me to help him construct a wooden raft so that on hot days, we could jump off it into to the lake to cool down. This ended up being an all-day project. After it was complete, we dragged it to the water's edge. As Steve pushed it out into the lake, Rick and I stood by, excited to try it out. Then to our disbelief, it sank before our eyes! Stunned and with great disappointment, we went back to work chopping weeds. We never did figure out what went wrong.

Between work and fun, we started to see improvements along the lake shore. The vision of a park started to become a reality before our eyes. Dad said, "One day we will name the park, but for now, there was still a lot more work to do."

Our summer was packed, full of adventure, work, and accomplishments. It also was a time of cherished family memories as unknown to us, this would be the last summer with our brother, Steve.

CHAPTER THREE

MY CROWDED HEART

THE LONG AWAITED FIRST DAY of high school finally arrived. I was starting seventh grade and feeling rather grown-up in my new plaid jumper and black fish net stockings. My brother Steve and I walked down our long dirt driveway to meet the bus. His long quick steps kept me skipping so I could keep up. Standing at the end of the driveway, my eye caught the bus coming down the road. Suddenly, I felt a tinge of nervousness inside, and my heart began to beat faster. I confessed to Steve that I was scared. "Ah, don't worry, it's no big deal," he said in his teenage demeanor.

Because I had always looked up to him, I was confident that he was right. The bus came to a stop, and I followed him up the steps, feeling proud that I was going to school with him.

Into the second quarter of school, I had adjusted to my schedule and made new friends. However, I began to feel overwhelmed as I was behind in my studies. Unknown to me, my learning skills were poor, and my self-esteem was lacking even more. Math was a giant hurdle. Then one day I was faced with a situation unpleasantly familiar, and I collapsed under the pressure. I was sitting in math class when my teacher, Mr. Wilson, called four students up to the blackboard. I was one of them. I stood up, recalling the experience a year ago like a bad dream. Panic quickly set in as I walked forward. Mr. Wilson had written a math equation for each of us on the board. I stood facing my math problem while the sound of chalk scratching on the board from the other students began to tease me.

Pressure built inside me as they each finished their problems and returned to their seats. My thought process totally shut down. I felt doomed!

Without as much as a mark on the board, I slowly set my chalk down and trembling, walked back to my seat, feeling the teacher's condemning look in my back and the other kids laughing inside. I closed my eyes and in moments, could hear Mr. Wilson coming up alongside my desk. Then as expected, he slapped my desk with his almighty ruler, causing me to jump with fear.

Looking at me, he said in a harsh tone, "Go back up there and do your equation."

With what little strength I had left within me, I barely managed to walk up the aisle, knowing every eye was on me. I quickly came to the realization that I could not face another moment. Succumbing to my emotions, I turned my back to the blackboard and walked straight out of the classroom. In the hall, I leaned against the wall as my legs buckled, and I slid to the floor. There was nothing left within me. My eyes filled with tears as I determined for myself, "I'm so dumb!"

Then something inside me snapped. In an instant, hostility and rebellion mounted as I sat on the floor and declared, "I will never let this happen to me again!" I was ready to lash out.

Later that day I found Steve by his locker. He greeted me with a smile and a "hi." I responded with a smile and said nothing about what had happened to me earlier. Perhaps it was because I felt there was no need or maybe he would think less of me. Either way, his presence was all I needed to get me through the rest of the day. Because Mom and Dad were stressed with things at home that I could not understand, I kept silent and never told them either.

For years, my dad would repeatedly tell me and my brothers we were "dumbbells." So it was powerfully confirmed "I didn't have an ounce of brains." Consequently, low self-esteem crept into my heart and took up residence like an angry, unwanted intruder.

The excitement grew all day as it was my thirteenth birthday, and I was having my girlfriends over for my first slumber party. Mom had prepared the snacks, and I planned the games. Every detail of my party was carefully thought out. Dad was going to be away for the night, so Mom gave me permission to stay up as late as we wanted. I was ecstatic.

The girls arrived with sleeping bags in tow, and soon the house was filled with giggling and laughter. Unexpectedly, Steve came home, and his cute teenage "presence" changed everything. The teasing and silliness between him and the girls were infuriating me! It was *my* birthday, and the girls were paying more attention to him than me.

"That's it!" I protested and stomped off to tell Mom. With frustration, I snapped, "Steve needs to leave! He's ruining my party!"

Mom said something to him, and before long, he made plans to get a ride into town from a neighbor boy and go to the school basketball game. Now, with no distractions, the rest of the night was filled with snacks, dancing, and laughter. I had waited a long time for this party, and I was having a blast.

Suddenly, the phone rang. I hesitated at answering it as we were in the middle of a game. Then I jumped up, still laughing as I ran to the phone in the kitchen. The man on the other end sounded serious. He asked if a parent was there. I quickly motioned for the girls to calm down and be quiet. I called for my mom to come to the phone. Standing by her side, I was stunned as her body sagged like the life was draining out of her.

Steve had been in a car accident. An ambulance was taking him to a trauma center in Minneapolis. The police officer told her to get to the hospital right away. Dad was called, and he was on his way. Mom called Grandma, and she quickly headed to our house. Mom left, leaving me with a sinking, empty feeling. All thoughts of the party vaporized.

I sat motionless, clinging to Steve's picture that I had taken off the wall. One at a time, the girls were being picked up by their parents. I hardly noticed when the last one left. During the night, I fought to keep my eyes open, hoping to stay awake until I heard some news. The attempt was futile—I fell asleep.

It was morning when I was awakened by movement on the foot of the bed. I opened my eyes and saw Rick was sitting there. The sun was coming in the window behind him, making me squint, but I could see he was crying.

"Barb, Steve died." He choked on the words as he sat limply.

Every part of me became numb, and I could not speak. Rick stayed sitting as I slowly stood and went upstairs to my grandma. Words froze in my mouth. Again, I could not speak. I went back to my room and sat on the edge of my bed. At that moment, the realization hit me. It was my fault—I made him leave.

Days had passed since the funeral, and I still hadn't cried. One day Mom confronted me with an angry tone. "Why don't you cry?"

I could not tell her about the burden I carried. Besides that, I was terrified of what Dad would say. No, I had to keep this to myself. However, days later, my world changed—it was Christmas, and I wanted my brother back. I broke down and sobbed.

During the next months, our home was filled with grief and silence. There was no discussion about Steve's death, resulting in little or no healing for me. And so guilt crept into my heart, telling my low self-esteem to move over. Thus, "low self-esteem" and "guilt" took up residence in my heart.

My brother Steven

Name of park on farm named after Steven.

For the next year and a half, my grades continued to fall. With no help from the school or from my grieving parents, I started to fail classes. Added to this, Rick and I endured our dad's anger toward the young man who was driving when Steve was killed. We could not do anything right for him. We displeased him unintentionally in everything we did. Meanwhile, Mom dealt with her own sadness and, for the first time, started working a part-time job outside the home.

I was fifteen when Dad and his friend, Bill, agreed that Bill would lease our barn and pasture so that he could raise horses on our farm. Bill, along with his two sons, would then help take care of our two horses since Steve was gone. With summer in full swing, weekends had become busier on the farm. Rick and I enjoyed the extra people around, which also seemed to make Dad a little happier.

Bill, who was a sixth-grade teacher, owned a cabin up in Northern Minnesota. He and his sons, along with their friends went to the cabin frequently. It sounded like a haven for kids, and one day, much to my surprise, Bill invited Rick and me to go up to the cabin for the first time. With permission from Mom and Dad, Rick and I excitedly packed for the weekend. We had not been away for quite some time, so we were looking forward to the much-needed get-away.

After arriving at the cabin that was tucked in the middle of "nowhere," we settled in and enjoyed a simple dinner. Rick and Bill's sons sat playing cards, and I had just finished reading a chapter in a book when Bill announced it was late and time to hit the sack. I was tired and quickly got into my pajamas. With my sleeping bag in my arms, I scanned the room that had two full-size beds. Not knowing which bed Rick and I were to sleep in, I asked. With a slight smile, Bill answered that Rick and his son would sleep in one bed, and I would sleep in the other. Chuckling, he added, "If you don't bite me, I won't bite you."

Quickly but nervously, I spoke up. "I'm okay sleeping in the same bed with my brother."

Turning away as if he did not hear me, he made it clear what the sleeping arrangements were.

Laying out my sleeping bag as close to the wall as possible, I climbed in and zipped up. I was locked in my thoughts when the lights went out and the room was plunged into darkness. Later, after the boys were asleep, the zipper on my sleeping bag was slowly and deliberately unzipped, and I was not the one unzipping it. I fought to keep him away throughout the night while the boys slept. This man, who was our dad's trusted friend, took advantage of the situation, knowing all along what his intentions were.

In the morning, while Bill was outside, Rick could tell something was wrong. "What's wrong, Barb?" he asked.

I shared with the boys what had happened. Rick gasped. Bill's son, however, just shook his head as if this was no surprise. Within an hour, with hardly any words spoken, we were packed up and heading home. The first chance I got to talk to Rick alone, I begged, "Promise me you will not tell anyone ever!"

He reluctantly agreed.

So "low self-esteem" and "guilt" naturally moved over to make room for "shame." Little did I know that, together, the deadly trio was going to slowly pierce my heart and silently kill my spirit. Ultimately, I became void of any self-worth, which caused me to give up. I soon found myself heading down a road of destruction.

CHAPTER FOUR

DO NOT ENTER

IF THERE WERE A SIGN that read "DO NOT ENTER," I would not have thought twice about entering! As a matter of fact, I would not have thought once about it—entering would have been a reflex. At fifteen, I was all about having fun, proving myself, and undermining authority. Rebellion stirred within me. Yet I showed genuine love, kindness, and was sensitive to the needs of others. My life was certainly confusing.

Because money was still tight at home—it always was—asking for it was usually out of the question. Besides, I grew to fear asking for *anything*. It was demeaning just to ask for school lunch money because my dad would make me feel like I was asking for too much. In time, I learned how to get things without having to ask for money, but only if I did not get caught. One day, while shoplifting—a nice way to say stealing—I *was* caught.

One day it was decided between a few friends and me that instead of going to school, it would be more fun to go "shopping." Soon we jumped into the car of one of the girls and headed for the store. When we arrived, we split up, each going our own way. We agreed to meet back at the car in thirty minutes. Although I did not need anything in particular, I snatched a shirt and some makeup, shoving them into my oversized purse.

Deep down, I knew what I was doing was wrong. Guilt cast its shadow over me, convicting me many times; but I simply reasoned my way past it, finding ways to justify my stealing. Suddenly, I realized that thirty minutes had gone by, and as planned, I left the store to meet up with my friends at the car. While walking out to the parking lot, I was unaware that I was being followed by store security. Waving happily to the girls, I noticed a man in uniform coming toward the car. As I turned to escape, I ran into the guys who were right behind me! We were caught. The ride downtown to the Minneapolis police station was long, which gave us time to think. The girls whispered among themselves about how scared they were. The only fear I had is what my dad was going to do to me.

Thankfully, it was my mom who came to pick me up. No charges were filed. Our parents were to deal with our punishment. We were permitted to leave after a police officer spoke with each of us. Then walking out of the police station, Mom asked where my jacket was because the day was chilly. "I don't have one," I answered.

Several minutes later, unexpectedly, Mom pulled into a shopping mall parking lot. She took me in to shop for a coat! After we purchased the navy-blue pea-coat, Mom suggested we go out for lunch. This was a rare treat that I truly did not think I deserved. Again, life had taught me that I did not deserve anything, but in this case, I felt it was true; however, I did enjoy it.

On our way home, Mom lovingly pointed out how stealing can hurt us. She expressed her concern for me. Mom always had a big heart, but she was saddened by my choice to steal. Although under bad circumstances, the uninterrupted time I got to spend with my mom comforted and assured me of her love. At that moment in time, something inside me changed. I never shoplifted again. During this time, Dad was struggling in the barber business. Because of this, it was necessary for me to work so I could pay for the things I needed. At sixteen, I got my first job waitressing in town.

Along with the struggles in my life were the struggles that our country was facing. Uncertainty, fear, anger, and death continued to heighten as the Vietnam War was taking its toll on our country, our state, and the communities where we lived. Everyone was affected in one way or another. That was very evident one night as I listened to my parents talk. My cousin had just come home from the war. Dad said, "He came back a different person."

My concern for my cousin caused me to question, "Why?"

My dad answered, "Because war does that to people who have fought in it."

I closed my eyes that night, fearing how Bobby might be "different." I did not know what to expect.

War was not the only crisis at the time. Along with it came something that would also plague our nation—drugs. Drug use was becoming widespread, and our small town was not spared its ravages. As a matter of fact, you could obtain anything you wanted with just a simple phone call. Sometimes you did not need to make a call—drugs were being sold right out of vehicles and students' lockers at school.

The drug scene came at an inopportune time, a time when I was most vulnerable to its alluring seductive qualities. It helped numb those destructive feelings that had taken up residence in my heart. I often sat in school with my head in a cloud from using one drug or another. My way of coping with my life and its betrayals was to get high. My way of dealing with life with my dad was to be high at home as well. In the meantime, no one ever stepped in and offered to help with my failing grades, nor did I ever ask for it.

Outside of school and away from home, my life was a party. It was part of the road I traveled that became very rocky, steep, and sometimes treacherous. But all the while, I enjoyed the protection "that life" gave me, like a Band-Aid over a wound. Getting high gave me the permission I needed to have fun—in an irrational way. Consuming alcohol was right up there with drugs and all the same reasons as the drugs.

In most towns, there is a place where young people like to congregate. Buffalo also had such a place, although not by its own choosing. It was a place to find out where the parties were or a place to hang out *and* party. The young people called it wide street. You would often see the townspeople driving by, either shaking their heads or cringing. My dad would complain, "Those dumb hippies with all their long hair!"

This was the place where I hung out, mostly on weekends with my long-haired friends.

"What!" I gasped, my mouth hanging open. "You're pregnant? Mom, you're too old!" was my initial response.

She just nodded and smiled. I did not know if I should celebrate with excitement or cry in disbelief. But seven months later, on April Fools' Day, Mom, at forty-one, gave birth to my baby sister, and I was ecstatic! Just like I did with my first sister, I got to name her. "Her name will be Kimberly," I announced proudly.

Like a kaleidoscope with endless patterns changing with each turn, my life's circumstances mirrored the changes but without the beauty. I soon faced a situation that abruptly changed the course of my life forever.

As I was growing up, my family attended a Lutheran church in town. I recall feeling like it was a good place to go, though I have no memory of ever hearing about Salvation through Jesus Christ. While sitting through confirmation for three years, I cannot recall anything I heard. However, I do remember sitting next to a boy who was in my grade at school.

Dan was popular and well liked by everyone who knew him. His flirty ways always gave the girls something to smile about. So when he started teasing me, that alone made it worth sitting through boring classes.

It was not until our junior year in high school that Dan approached me out of the blue and asked me to go with him to the school's fall dance. Totally surprised, all I could do was stand there and stare at him as he waited for my answer. Finally, awkwardly, I managed to answer a "yes." Shortly after, we began dating.

One night, as I was running out the front door to hop into Dan's car, he stopped me and asked if he could come in and meet my parents. Suddenly, I was nervous and started stammering. Was my fear because Dan had long hair, or was it because I never knew what Dad was going to say? I was just sure the meeting would not go well. Hesitantly, I turned around and invited him into the house. Much to my relief, I could soon tell that Dad approved of Dan—long hair and all! However, it was not until the next day when Mom confided in me Dad's car had stalled along the road a while back and a young man pulled over to help him. That young man just happened to be Dan!

I flipped the page in my calendar over, and over again, trying to remember my last period. In February, I had missed another one. By this time, my friend would have to get off the school bus with me in the middle of nowhere because I had morning sickness. We would then walk the rest of the way to school. It was not long, and I was becoming aware of changes in my body. Still in denial, I wanted to make sense of the changes, so I skipped lunch one day, went to the library, and found a book on reproduction. Afraid of being discovered, I found a quiet area behind some bookshelves and sat down to read. Within moments, I felt like butterflies were swirling around inside me. Another wave of nausea hit me.

A friend's elder sister suggested that Dan and I go to a Planned Parenthood office in Minneapolis. There, we could have a pregnancy test done in secret. I made the appointment, still hoping my nausea was caused by something else. The day of the appointment found me nervously fidgeting with my sweater, waiting for the results of my test. A doctor came in with the news. My hopes of the flu were crushed. At just seventeen, I was pregnant! Overwhelmed, I began to cry. Wanting Dan by my side, I asked if he could come into the consultation room with me. The man answered a brusque "no" and left the room. Within minutes, a woman came in, shutting the door behind her. She explained that she was a counselor and that she wanted to discuss my situation.

"What do you want to do with your pregnancy?" she asked.

Confused, I said, "What do you mean?"

She repeated herself, and it soon became clear what she was asking me.

"My boyfriend and I decided that if I was pregnant, we would raise the baby together," I explained passionately.

Then as if she did not hear me, she deliberately pulled out a booklet and began to discuss "my options." "I know this is hard, but you could put the baby up for adoption, giving the responsibility to someone who's ready for it." Then before anything came out of my mouth, she said matter-of-factly, "Or you could have a procedure done so you wouldn't have to be pregnant anymore. It's called an abortion."

I jumped up, glaring at her, and snapped, "No one is going to touch this baby! It's mine!"

I stormed out of the room, not even shutting the door behind me. Never in my life have I ever questioned my decision.

The drive to Watertown, South Dakota, was long, but that is where we had to go to get married legally. In Minnesota, you had to be eighteen years old. When we came back home, our parents gave us a reception. Mom had sewed a simple white dress, and I wore daisies in my hair. It was all incredible, but reality had not sunk in yet.

Weeks before we had gotten married, a trailer house was set up on the dairy farm of Dan's family. The following day, after the wedding, the wedding gifts were put away. Exhausted, I sat staring at a pile of homework, knowing that it would be back to school tomorrow. Suddenly, I felt as though my life was like a book and a chapter was skipped, resulting in a confusing storyline. I continued staring at the homework in front of me while my mind was trying to grasp that I was now a wife and soon-to-be mother.

Summer vacation could not have come soon enough. At six months, my tummy was starting to really pop out. Vacation from school gave me the time to prepare for the baby. Instantly, I began to love life on the farm, even helping with milking the cows in the parlor. Fall arrived way too quickly; I was three days from my due date. With no control over the timing of things, I grew concerned as school was starting in one week. Dan and I would begin our senior year of high school—possibly as parents.

It was September, the first day of school, when our classmates began their senior year, and I gave birth to a baby boy. We named him Jeremy. Quickly, after Dan held his son, he ran from the room. I found out later he went to school, and over the loudspeaker, he announced, "I just had a son!"

Meanwhile, the students clapped and cheered as the teachers laughed because of the way he said it.

Three months later, Dan's mother announced she was expecting. So at one year old, my son, Jeremy, had an aunt (my baby sister) who was a year older and now another aunt who was a year younger than he was.

Dan and I were fortunate to have his mother care for Jeremy so that we could finish our last year of high school. Then finally, with celebration on graduation day, with Dan holding our son, we walked down the aisle to receive our diplomas as a family.

During our first year, it became increasingly difficult to maintain a relationship, let alone a marriage. Although we loved our son and took good care of him, Dan and I, being kids ourselves, fought constantly.

It was late winter, and once again, I could feel restlessness building up in Dan. Then one day he announced, "I am going to Mexico. If you want to go, you will need your passport."

Soon our van was packed for the two-week trip. Because I could not leave Jeremy alone for that long, another bag was packed. Jeremy was four years old.

Traveling through Mexico was an adventure, to say the least. The terrain was rugged, and the language barrier was a challenge. There was also concern for our safety. Dan kept reminding me that he had brought a gun, which scared me even more. As we drove into Mexico City, I breathed a sigh of relief. We also longed for a hot meal and shower. After checking into the hotel, we anxiously went to our room. Upon entering, we stopped in our tracks. The worn-out linoleum floor was not the only thing that caught our attention, but also a cockroach the size of a cat that scurried across the floor! After settling in and taking lukewarm showers, we set out to find dinner. The night was long, and there was little sleep as the springs in the mattress poked us like daggers.

The next day we stood in amazement as we looked up at Mexico's largest pyramid. Jeremy and I climbed its ancient steps and got halfway up. Dan, however, continued to climb to the top, so far up we could barely see him because of the clouds.

Dan rarely drove on main highways; we came to a small village that was far off the beaten path. Local kids ran up to our van in excitement. It felt good to get out and stretch. Earlier, Dan had given Jeremy a handful of bubble gum. He was told to share it with the kids. Hands were reaching as Jeremy handed out the gum. I quickly noticed the kids touching the top of Jeremy's head. Laughing and speaking Spanish, the kids surrounded him. Suddenly, it occurred to us they were interested in his white-blond hair. We took out our camera to catch the moment.

On the road again, we drove south to Acapulco, where we swam in the aqua-blue Pacific Ocean and walked the white sandy beaches. To our surprise, we began noticing armed men walking the beaches as well. It was scary to realize that they were guerilla fighters or drug dealers. Anxious to get moving, we packed up and drove inland toward the Sierra Madres Mountains. This was an uncharted area of the country in which two young Americans with a four-year-old child had no business being. This was the beginning of a "vacation gone bad."

I felt uneasy as we traveled up into the mountains. The roads became rougher, and civilization seemed to disappear. Pulling off the road one night to sleep, I said, "This is crazy!"

Dan slept with the gun at his side. Before the light of dawn, we were back on the road again.

It was lunchtime, and I pulled out some crackers to snack on. Suddenly, unexpectedly, we could see in the distance a guarded checkpoint on the road! Dan yelled, "Get the pot out of the heater and hide it!"

Not knowing that he brought two pounds of marijuana with us, I quickly replied, "Where?"

Then as two gunmen, one on each side, walked toward our van, waving their M16 rifles in the air, I frantically fought to pull the back of the heater off. Almost at once, I tucked the pot underneath my shirt and pushed the back of the heater on just as our van rolled to a stop. Suddenly, the doors of the van were pulled open on both sides. Grabbing Jeremy with one arm and holding the pot tightly under my shirt with the other, we were ordered to get out. Dan was quickly ushered away. Jeremy and I were taken off to the side of the road. I imagined that they were going to body search Dan, and I would probably be next.

Some of the men immediately began to search our van. They dismantled everything, including the heater. I stood with my arms tightly crossed. Beads of sweat dripped down my face. Jeremy clung to my side and, thankfully, remained quiet. A guard stood on the other side of me, holding his gun as if I were going to run. I watched in horror as they emptied out our van.

It was not long before Dan was ushered back to where we were waiting. I was told by an interpreter that a woman guard would be coming for me. Dan and I looked at each other, knowing we were in serious trouble. Unknown to us at the time, a five-year prison term was imposed for this type of crime. That meant prison in Mexico!

Suddenly, Jeremy started to cry. Dan picked him up to comfort him. It seemed like hours when the interpreter finally came back, telling the guard something we could not understand. Moments later, he came over to me and said, "Ma'am, the woman guard is nowhere to be found. Your body search is called off." Then he added, "We don't want to frighten the little boy any longer." He told us we could leave.

With no offer of help from the guards, we were left alone to put our van back together. All the while, I awkwardly moved my arms as not to arouse suspicion. Then as we finished, the interpreter came over to tell us that they confiscated the gun, and we could not have it back. It would be sent to a government building an hour away. He advised us to leave and head back North. Soon after we left the checkpoint, it occurred to me that Dan had not turned the van around to go North. Surprised, he told me to return the pot back to its hiding spot in the heater. Fearful of getting stopped again, I yelled, "No!"

Before he could say another word, I rolled my window down and threw out the pot. The van slammed to a halt, and I paid dearly for my action.

Lying on the floor of the van, my body hurt at every bump in the road. Jeremy slept, and Dan kept driving. I did not have to guess as to where we were headed. I knew he would not leave Mexico without his gun. I assumed by this time that we were close to the government building where we would wait for his gun. I slowly came up front to sit. We had not said a word to each other. Then just as if I were in a bad dream, I noticed burned-out trucks and cars along the roadside. Something inside me felt like things were not right. Looking up onto the hillsides, we could see small groups of armed men standing behind or near fort-like walls made from boulders. Slowly and cautiously, we arrived at a building in the middle of nowhere in Mexico.

Tense from driving, Dan jumped out of the van and walked toward the building. Afraid to stay in the van alone, I grabbed Jeremy and followed him. As we walked in, a man from behind the counter stared at us as if in shock. At once, he said in broken English, "Did you kids drive up here by yourselves?"

We nodded "yes."

With his eyes bulging from his head, he barked, "You drove through a combat zone! There is fighting in these hills—you could have been blown up!"

That explained all the burned-out vehicles. Dan explained to him about his gun. Calming down, the man continued, "You cannot stay here to wait for your gun. You need to leave."

He called for security so that we could be escorted out safely.

You would think that if two people could make it through this, they could make it through anything. But after we returned home from Mexico, I came to the sad realization that we could not withstand the pressures of marriage. As deep as love can get between two young kids, we knew that things would not get any easier. With all the amazing talent and goodness in Dan, also came an addiction to drugs and alcohol. They changed him into something he was not.

In the end, I am thankful for my relationship with Dan. If it were not for that part of my life's journey, I would not have my wonderful son Jeremy.

My siblings (I am holding Kimberly), Rick and Nancy.
I am pregnant with Jeremy.

Mexico City: Jeremy after sharing bubble gum with children.

CHAPTER FIVE

BEYOND WHAT'S
BROKEN

SOON AFTER I MOVED AWAY from the farm of Dan's parents, I started working a job at a textile warehouse. Needing a place to live, I rented a quaint little house with one of my coworkers, Paula. The house, located in a lake-community area, was perfect for us. It had a room off the kitchen for Jeremy.

Along with the new job came new friends and a whole new environment away from Dan. Significant circumstances changed as well. Jeremy was growing up and had started school. I was now learning how to budget my money for the first time. As a single mom, I was forced to make responsible decisions every day, and things in my life seemed to be settling down. Then in one day's time, I saved someone's life, came to the aid of another, and kept myself from murdering someone else! The chain of events started early one morning, after dropping Jeremy off at day care as I drove to work.

Taking the outside of a wide curve in the road, I noticed a car coming toward me from the opposite direction in the middle of the road! Then before I could react, my car was hit in the rear fender, spinning it out of control. After both cars came to a stop, the driver of the other car and I got out. He was just as stunned as I was. We could quickly see that no one was hurt.

"I just got off the night shift—I must have fallen asleep!" he blurted.

My heart still pounding, we turned and looked at the curve. At that moment, we began to realize what would have happened if the collision with my car had not been there to stop his. No doubt he would have been killed, flying over the steep embankment and ending up in the trees at the bottom. I walked back to my car, amazed to find that there was only a smashed taillight and the bumper peeled back. I stood staring at my car with mixed emotions—thankful that no one was seriously hurt but devastated to have been in an accident. I had just picked my car up from a repair shop the day before because of another accident that I had been in. After we exchanged information, the man secured the bumper to my car with a rope he happened to have.

As I continued my drive to work, I replayed the accident over and over in my mind. That afternoon, while on my lunch break, a coworker asked me if I wanted to go for a quick ride on his new motorcycle. Not really in the mood, but not wanting to hurt his feelings, I said, "Okay, just a quick ride."

I hopped onto the back of his bike and held on tight as he took off, going way too fast for my comfort. We went around the block and then headed back to the warehouse. As we came around the corner, he suddenly yelled, "Hold on!"

Unknown to me, he decided to jump a large pile of sand in the parking lot! He immediately lost control, and we landed sideways, crashing to the ground. I fell to the side of the bike with part of my leg under it. The bike was pulled forward by the momentum of the crash, pinning me so I could not get up. I immediately felt pain in my leg, but I was sure it was not broken. Anger churned inside me as I managed to get out from under the bike and to my feet. I snapped, "Why did you do that?"

Without waiting for an answer, I limped into the building to get away from him; at that moment, I really wanted to murder him.

Late that afternoon, I punched out of work and limped back out to my "wrecked" car. All I could think about was how I wanted to just go home, relax, and try to make sense of my day. Although I was mentally tired and physically hurting, it felt good to get home. I poured myself a glass of lemonade and walked into the living room to sit down when the doorbell rang. Squinting in pain, I turned to answer the door. A boy who looked to be eleven or twelve was standing there. He smiled and reminded me that I had hired him to mow the lawn. I told him to go ahead but to be careful. With that warning, I limped back to the living room to sit down.

Several minutes had gone by when I realized that I had not heard the mower running. It seemed a little strange, but I remained there resting. Suddenly, the doorbell rang again. I got up slowly because of the pain and went to the door. As I opened it, I could hear the boy crying. There he stood, holding his hand, bleeding onto his pants and shoes. While pulling him into the house, I glanced at the mower which was tipped on its side. From years of mowing lawn on the farm, I immediately knew what had happened. With tears streaming down his face, he told me he was turning the blade to clean it. I rushed him over to the kitchen sink and ran cool water over his hand. To my horror and trying to do the best that I knew how, I tightly wrapped his hand in a wet towel. He needed medical attention fast!

I was thankful when he told me that he only lived two blocks away and that his mother was home. To my dismay, when we got there, she had no car. She told me to take the boy to his dad's office—only blocks away. She would call him and let him know we were on the way. I asked if she could come with, and she said no. Back in the car, the boy begged me not to bring him to his dad.

Arriving at the office, I did not get four steps away from my car when the Dad walked up and started yelling at the boy for doing such an unwise thing. He shouted, "I do not have time for this!"

With no concern at all, he handed me his insurance card. Then unexpectedly, he gave me directions to the hospital—in another town ten miles away! I was so dumbfounded I was at a loss for words. I looked over at the boy who was now crying. I did not have time to wonder why a dad wouldn't care about his son; we had to go and go fast.

Driving down the highway, I gripped the stirring wheel so hard my knuckles turned white. With every bump in the road, my car's bumper thumped from just being tied on with a rope, and my leg thumped even more. Once again, the boy began to cry, not as much from the pain, but because he was so afraid of what his dad would do when he got home. My heart broke for the boy.

"Where is the hospital?" I said to myself silently, not wanting to scare the boy by letting him know I was scared. "Am I even on the right road?" I questioned myself.

I glanced at the boy and noticed that there was blood. I sighed with relief as I spotted the small community hospital up ahead. We had finally arrived after what seemed like hours.

As soon as we walked in, a nurse came to take the boy. But to my surprise, he grabbed for my hand. He wanted me to stay by his side. I quickly assured him that I would come back after I talked to the receptionist. My eyes followed him until he disappeared around the corner. The lady behind the counter held up the insurance card and asked, "Where are his parents?"

Again, I had to explain what had happened as she could not comprehend what I was telling her. Then as promised, I went to find the boy.

Two hours had passed, and because the parents had never called to check on the boy, the doctor told me he would call them. I assumed he not only wanted to give them care instructions for their son's injury, but also to give them some words about parental responsibility.

"Can you stay with me at my house?" the boy cried softly, pleading with me as I drove him home.

"I can't." The words barely came out of my mouth.

Then feelings of dread overcame me as I pulled up to the curb. In front of us stood his dad, puffing on the last of a cigarette. He showed no signs of gladness or compassion as he flicked the butt to the ground. Suddenly, fear enveloped me as I recalled my own feelings from childhood. I whispered to the boy to "be brave."

We got out, and with no more than a quick, cold "thank you," the dad took the insurance card from my hand and marched the boy up the steps to the apartment building. With a heavy heart, I got back in my car and drove home.

After pulling into my driveway, I sat in my car reflecting on this awfully long very traumatic day. I finally got out of the car and shut the door. The bumper fell off and hit the ground with a clang. I slowly limped into the house. My head hurt, my leg throbbed, but it was my heart that really ached; for the boy I had just come to know who was so afraid.

Two months passed before I saw him again. I was glad to see that his finger had healed. When I asked him how it went that night after I had dropped him off, he shrugged and said he did not want to talk about it. I never saw him again.

It has been many years since that time, and I wonder whatever happened to that boy. I hope that someday our paths will cross again.

CHAPTER SIX

NIGHTMARE ON FOURTH STREET

IT SEEMS MY LIFE'S JOURNEY has been one adventure and challenge after another. But along the way, I've learned many difficult life lessons. One day one lesson nearly had me doubting my capability to be a good mother.

The time had come for me to look for a sitter for Jeremy while I worked. He was now five years old. It was suggested that I go to the nearby grocery store to see if anyone had posted offers to provide childcare services. Immediately, I found information on the bulletin board. I was excited to see that one child-care provider lived near my home. I wrote the telephone number down and called her when I got home. A meeting was set up for the next day.

Pulling up to the curb, I looked down at the address again. I was surprised to be sitting in front of an apartment building. The woman had advertised that she did child-care in her home. I wrestled with going in as I was unsure of this kind of arrangement. But then I considered how convenient the location was. I parked the car, and I went in. I noticed immediately that the apartment was clean, and the children's things were tidy. The woman seemed to be nice. She told me she was currently caring for two other children. Again, thinking about the convenience, I decided to hire her.

Monday morning, I was surprised when the woman met me and Jeremy down at the entrance to the apartment building. I found this odd as we had planned that I would bring Jeremy up to the apartment, but I was in a hurry to get to work, so I did not question it. After some brief words were said, I bent down to kiss Jeremy goodbye, whispering for him to mind his manners. I drove to work with a strong feeling of uneasiness in the pit of my stomach.

At work, I thought often about Jeremy. I looked forward to going home and hearing about his day. After work, I drove to the sitter to pick him up. As I walked down the hall, I noticed that the door to the apartment was slightly open. Peeking in, I could see the woman sitting on the couch with a cigarette in one hand and a beer in the other. The television was blaring. Scanning the room, I was surprised to see it was in horrible disarray, unlike the day I had stopped over to meet her. The mess was probably why she had met us downstairs, at the front door, that morning. Suddenly, I grew very anxious.

I knocked on the door and got no response. I knocked louder. The woman turned and looked toward me but not *at* me. I knew instantly she had been drinking a lot. Feeling impatient, I asked where Jeremy was. She stared at me as if she did not hear me. I asked again. Then in slurred speech, she "guessed" that he may be playing outside with the other kids. Without saying another word to her, I turned and ran down the hall, calling his name. When I got outside, I found the kids playing.

"Where is Jeremy?" I asked the other kids.

They shrugged, and one girl finally said they had not seen him for a long time. Trying to keep myself together, I ordered the kids to go tell the babysitter that Jeremy was missing. Then with a puzzled look, the eldest child said, "Oh, that's not our babysitter, that's our mom."

I quickly realized that the woman had lied about doing child-care for other children. I had to push my anger aside and focus on finding my son. Then suddenly, it occurred to me that he could have walked home! That was my only hope. My heart pounded as I raced down the street to my house. Jumping out of my car, I ran to the door. It was locked! I headed to the backyard. As I came around the corner of the house, I spotted him sitting in his sandbox, oblivious to the world around him. I stopped and took a deep breath, then slowly let it out. Wiping the tears from my face, I walked up to the sandbox and sat down next to Jeremy.

Running my fingers through his blond hair, I asked, "Jeremy, why did you leave the babysitter?"

While pushing his car through the sand, he said, "I didn't like her, and I wanted to go home."

I sat motionless, pouring over the mistakes I had made in choosing the babysitter and what could have happened to him if he had not found his way home.

The next day I drove back to the grocery store and pulled the woman's ad off the bulletin board. The whole time I wrestled with thoughts of being a bad mom. Although it was clear that I was a young mom with a lot to learn, I was wrong to assume that all people can be trusted. Ultimately, I concluded—she was a bad mom, and *I* was a good mom to my son! I soon found a new sitter, and Jeremy loved her.

The first year of living on my own flew by quickly. Although things seemed to be going well in my life, I still struggled with the things from the past that constantly crushed my heart. Low self-esteem continued to judge me as dumb, while shame and guilt echoed in my mind. My birthdays were a time of celebration but a sad reminder of the brother I dearly missed. It was during this time that I was told that Mom was enduring Dad's anger toward life's difficulties. Rick had left home and moved out West, and we would not hear from him for quite some time. Bitterness toward my dad mounted.

Despite the storms in my life, I faced each day with a ray of hope for a better tomorrow. After all, I now had the responsibility of raising my son. Jeremy was now enduring the hardships of a broken family. He lived with me throughout the week and with Dan every other weekend. Dan always looked forward to picking up his son. I resented the void inside me every time Jeremy left.

I had grown to love the little cottage-like house that Paula and I had rented. It sat on a quiet street with lots of trees. Besides the vacant lot across the street, our house was surrounded by larger older homes. It was peaceful. But on one unusually hot day, I experienced a nightmare that rocked my quiet, peaceful refuge.

I scooted Jeremy out the door as the school bus came to a stop. I waved goodbye and then waved at Paula as she left to go to work. I had taken the day off and was looking forward to having the house to myself. By early afternoon, the temperature outside was sweltering. The house was getting uncomfortably warm, so I closed the doors and windows and turned on the air-conditioner.

Because I worked at a textile warehouse, I had lots of fabric on hand. I decided to set my sewing machine up on the kitchen table and start sewing a skirt. Hours passed, and the hum of the machine was comforting as the fabric slid across the push plate. Suddenly, I thought I heard a noise, I stopped the machine and listened. I heard it again! I knew that Jeremy would not be home from school for another half hour. I did not expect Paula home for another forty-five minutes.

My attention was drawn to the door just off the kitchen. From where I was sitting, I could see the doorknob jiggling. I froze! The door slowly opened up, and a man's figure appeared in the doorway! He quickly stepped in, shutting the door behind him. I saw that he was wearing a black leather jacket and gloves. A stocking cap was pulled down to his eyebrows. He never took his eyes off me. Confused and scared, I tried to make sense of what was happening. Things just did not feel right. Wearing a leather jacket and gloves in this temperature certainly wasn't "normal." I also did not recall hearing the rumble of a motorcycle. He took a few steps toward me when, suddenly, something inside me woke, and I quickly went into survival mode. With my eyes slowly looking down, I took note of where my scissor and seam ripper were lying.

The man asked, as if confused, "Are you Betty?"

Shaking, I answered, "No, my name is Barb."

In an angry voice, he snapped, "You are a liar!"

Again, I repeated my name. He moved slowly toward me and then stopped. I focused on my scissor, waiting for him to make his next move. He demanded that I tell him my real name. I knew something was terribly wrong. He paced back and forth and was soon behind me. I turned toward him and asked, "What do you want from this Betty?"

Sweat trickled down my forehead as I waited for his answer. He stopped beside me, reached into his pocket, and pulled out a razor cutter. I pleaded my identity and offered to show him proof.

What had seemed like hours since he first came into the house was only minutes. It became clear, the more I pleaded, the more nervous and confused he seemed. I was also aware that Jeremy would be coming through the door at any moment. I sat still as my mind gathered a plan of attack. The man kept one eye on me and the other searching through the papers on the counter. Then suddenly, the door opened, and there stood Jeremy! The man ordered me to stay sitting in the chair. He seemed wound tighter than a spring. He yanked the phone cord from the wall.

"I will not hurt the boy if you stay sitting in that chair. I just want to talk to him."

Then he took Jeremy into the room just off the kitchen and shut the door. Within seconds, as I struggled with what to do, in walked Paula!

With the look of horror on my face, Paula intuitively knew something was wrong. I pointed to the closed door and whispered, "Help."

Without any questions, Paula flung the door open. Jeremy was sitting on the edge of the bed, where the man was questioning him. The man jumped in surprise. He took one look at Paula, pushed past her, and ran out the door.

After the police were called, it occurred to us that we had neither heard nor seen any vehicle outside. The man just vanished!

Months passed while I tried to erase that incident from my mind. But now every time I heard a noise, I froze! Then one day, like an episode out of a scary movie, I read some disturbing news in the Minneapolis newspaper. I came across an article that talked about a body that was found on a vacant lot in the area where I lived. To my amazement, it was reported that a woman was found dead there. She had been murdered, and her name was Betty!

CHAPTER SEVEN

MY TESTIMONY

I HAD BEEN WORKING AT the textile warehouse for two years when I noticed a new face in the warehouse. His tall frame and dark brown hair stood out from the other workers; but it was his smile that really caught my eye. On his third day of work, I felt really drawn to meet him. To cover up my real intentions, I gathered some bolts of fabric in my arms, so it would seem that I had another purpose in approaching him. I walked nervously over to his station. When our eyes met, he smiled and stopped what he was doing. The bolts of fabric in my arms were forgotten as we introduced ourselves. After a brief conversation, I turned to go back to my station. Curious wonder mixed with a strong sense of physical desire overcame me. Then later-on in the day, something extraordinary happened while on my lunch break.

The horn had sounded for lunch. Employees either went outside or to the break room to eat. I quickly looked around to see where the new guy, Ed, was going. He was nowhere to be seen. Disappointed, I sat down in the break room and opened my lunch. Then to my surprise, I spotted him at the other end of the long break room table. Barely able to eat, from the corner of my eye, I watched him talk and laugh with some of his coworkers. Suddenly, as if someone whispered in my ear, I heard, "Someday you're going to marry that man."

Fidgeting with my sandwich, I quickly looked around the table to see if anyone else heard what I had heard. It was so real! When I looked back at him, our eyes met, and he smiled. I knew instantly in my heart that what had just happened *was* real! It did not take long before coworkers began to detect hearts floating above us every moment we were together.

One day, while at work, Ed invited me to meet him and a friend at a dance club. I accepted, but not wanting to go alone, I immediately called a friend. That night we drank, laughed, and danced until the last call and last dance were announced. The evening had gone by way too fast, and we were not ready to say good night as we had so much more to talk about. Late into the night, Ed and I sat in an all-night restaurant enjoying coffee, breakfast, and each other. It was clear that our lives were on a path of convergence, moving toward something greater than what we had experienced so far.

At this point in my life, I continued to party and smoke pot—but never in the presence of my son. Also, Ed was drawn to and hung around with people into the party and drug scene. His friend, Tom, was heavily involved in dealing and using drugs. Unexpectedly, something happened to Tom. To Ed's surprise, Tom became a "born-again" Christian and soon noticed that Tom's life began to change. In time, because of Tom's boldness to share his new faith, Ed and I were faced with a decision that would change our lives.

It had been a busy week at work, so by the time the weekend arrived, Ed and I were ready to party. Arriving at the dance club, we found an empty booth. We ordered drinks, and in moments, they were in front of us. Ed picked up his drink to take a sip when he slowly set his glass down. Curious, I followed the gaze of his eyes to see what had caught his attention. It was his friend, Tom, and he was walking toward us. I had not met him yet, then I saw Ed force a smile, making me wonder what was going on. Ed introduced us, and to my surprise, Tom asked, "Ed, could I talk with you out in my car?"

With a questioning look on his face, Ed took a swallow of his drink and stood up. Tom turned to me and invited me to join them. I followed, assuming we were going out to the car to smoke some pot.

Thirty minutes had gone by while the guys carried on a casual conversation. The more I sat and listened, the more annoyed I got. If we were not going to get high, I wanted to get back into the club and have fun. Frustrated, I lit up a cigarette. Suddenly, there was a pause in the conversation. Tom cleared his throat, and in a serious tone, he said, "Ed, do you want to go with me to the Jesus People Church in Downtown Minneapolis tomorrow?" While Ed hesitated to answer, Tom turned to me and said, "Maybe you'd like to come too."

I had not been in a church service in years, and I knew Ed had not either. We had talked about this days earlier, agreeing that there is a God, and we felt like that was enough—we were okay. At any other time, I probably would have said no to the invitation, but suddenly, I felt compelled to accept. Ed looked at me, waiting for my response that would get him off the hook. That did not happen. I nodded and said, "We should go."

The night was then cut short so we would be able to get up in the morning instead of sleeping until noon. Ed took me home, kissed me good night and, laughed at our sudden change in plans.

The next morning I picked up Jeremy so that he could come with us. Tom greeted us with a smile as we entered the church. Waiting for the service to start, I sat anxiously waiting, feeling out of my comfort zone. Looking around at the assortment of people, young and old, homeless and rich, people of all colors and nationalities, I was in awe. I came from a small town where everyone knew everyone, and we all looked the same. To pass the time, Ed busied himself with Jeremy. Then the service began.

Music and singing filled the sanctuary. Hands were being lifted, and people began to speak out loud, which seemed out of place. Ed just looked at me and shrugged. The pastor began his sermon, talking about things I did not understand, like "salvation." I soon felt the need to pay close attention because the pastor was communicating something that I instinctively felt was especially important. I gave Jeremy a pencil and paper to keep him busy while I listened.

The message went something like this: The heart of Christianity is quite simple. It is a message from the Bible, about God and his son, Jesus. It is about life and death and the choice that we all must face. It starts with a loving God who created the world and everything in it. God made people rulers of the world, under only Him (Rev 4:11). But we all rejected God, ruling our lives, and rather wanting to do things our own way—without Him. We followed our own desires. The trouble is, in rejecting God, we made a mess, not only of our own lives, but also of our society and the whole world (Ro 3:10–12). But God will not let us rebel forever. His punishment for rebellion is death and judgment (Heb 9:27). It is a terrible thing to fall under the sentence of God's judgment. It is a prospect we all face since we are all guilty of rebelling against God, which is sin. Knowingly driving over the speed limit, taking more than what is ours, thinking lustful thoughts, or gossiping about someone—it is all sin. However, because of God's love for us, He sent his Son into the world—the man Jesus Christ. Jesus always obeyed what his Father said, so He did not deserve death or punishment. Yet Jesus died on the cross to pay the penalty for *our* sins (1 Pe 3:18). Then God raised Jesus to life again as Redeemer of mankind and Ruler of the world. Jesus conquered death by being raised from the dead so that we may live eternally with God (1 Pe 1:3). Jesus is our only way to God! One day Jesus will return to judge us for our earthly lives and actions (2 Co 5:10).

But until then, Jesus offers us new life, now and eternally. Our sins can be forgiven *now*. In this new life, God Himself comes to live within us by His Spirit–the Holy Spirit. We can now experience the joy of a new relationship with God. So there are two ways to live on this earth: our way, rejecting God and facing death; or His way, in which we submit to Jesus and live eternally with God (Jn 3:36).

The pastor stopped at these words and paused. Suddenly, I felt as though I were sitting in a court room, the jury was in, and the judge was reading my verdict: Guilty! I sat motionless. The pastor continued, and you could not ignore or mistake the sincerity in his voice. He boldly asked, "Which way do you want to live?"

Immediately, my eyes searched the hundreds of people around me, and I thought, *He is speaking directly to me!*

At this point, I realized the way I was living was not acceptable to God. The battle that raged in my heart and mind was piercing, draining the life from me. I wanted something right in my life!

Soon the pastor did something I had never heard of before. He challenged us to reach out to God through Jesus Christ. He then invited all those who wanted to make a decision to receive Christ into their lives to come up to the altar. In my mind, I did not question it. I wanted Jesus in my life. I wanted God's unconditional love and forgiveness. I needed forgiveness for myself. From all over the sanctuary, people began to walk up to the altar, the young and old, the homeless and rich, people of all colors and nationalities.

I was overcome. My heart pounded. Suddenly, unexpectedly, Ed and I stood to our feet at the same time! He smiled, took my hand, and we walked to the altar together. On that day, November 20, 1977, Ed and I received Christ into our lives. One year later, on the evening of a December blizzard, Ed and I were married with Jeremy by our side.

As God had planned, he put a fork into the road. Ed and I chose to follow the high road, wanting to change for the better. However, our marriage soon came upon bumpy roads, and it was not time to stop for a picnic either. Life took us on a journey through beautiful mountain peaks and down through dark difficult valleys.

Taken on our wedding day (1978)

CHAPTER EIGHT

THE HAMEL HOUSE

FIVE MONTHS AFTER OUR WEDDING day, our son Mike was born. Then two years later, our daughter Missy came along. My son, Jeremy, lived with us, visiting Dan every other weekend. During the summer months, he would spend more time at the farm of Dan's parents. Becoming a family of five so quickly in our marriage forced Ed and I to grow significantly. However, it was the demands of family, work, and life itself that would overshadow the unexpected mounting problems caused by living in a stepfamily. In later chapters, this will come to light.

Ed and I never lived in one place very long. Because we moved so often, boxes were usually broken down and saved, ready for the next departure. One day we got word of an old farmhouse for rent in the country. It sat outside the small town of Hamel, on Hamel Road. We moved in and stayed eight years in what we called the Hamel House.

With only a high school education, Ed began working for his brother's tree-removal service. During the winter months, he worked odd jobs wherever he could find them. I took on several small jobs: ironing clothes, babysitting, and cleaning homes. For the most part, I was content with being home with the kids. Following the old ways of thinking, I continued to view myself harshly—thoughts of being uneducated. Growing up, I had believed I was dumb. Some thought patterns take a long time to change. Because of my self-condemnation, I hesitated to step out into the working world. Obviously, we lived paycheck to paycheck, barely scraping by.

I was grateful that, as a child, I had learned how to cultivate and maintain a garden. The produce would help carry us through the winter months when money was especially tight. Ed's parents also taught us how to can and preserve fresh fruits, vegetables, and even meat. In spite of all the learning, I distinctly remember a disaster in the kitchen. During the process of cooking red beets in a pressure cooker, the cover apparently was not fastened correctly. It blew straight up into the air and the beets with it! The entire kitchen and everything in it were coated with red beet juice!

The Hamel House was a huge old two-story farm home, making it nearly impossible to heat properly. The second floor had a long hallway with three bedrooms on each side. To heat it better, we built a double-barrel wood-burning stove inside the house. Because Ed worked for the tree-removal service, we were well supplied with plenty of logs. We split and burned eight full cords of wood each winter. This drastically cut down what had been huge heating bills.

Adding to our ways of being resourceful, I did a lot of sewing—a talent that I acquired from my mom. I sewed most of my daughter's and my clothes. I also made curtains, tablecloths, pillows, and gifts. It became clear that, while I was not the most educated person, I was certainly creative and hardworking. Over time I discovered these qualities worked in a unique way to pay for essentials and put gas in my car.

One hot summer day, while driving down Hamel Road, I noticed a small children's picnic table sitting under a big oak tree. Slowing down to look at it, I thought, *I could build tables like that one for extra income.*

I pulled off to the side of the road to get a better look. In moments, I began to reminisce about a time during my junior year in high school.

With the second semester approaching quickly, I decided to switch from an economics class to a wood shop class. But there was one problem—shop was considered a "boys only" class. It was unheard of for a girl to be in *any* shop class. I signed up anyway. Soon after, the shop teacher confronted me and said, "It just won't work for you to be in my class."

I was so disappointed but not willing to give up. I went and spoke to the school counselor, and he was willing to discuss the situation with the principal. The next week I was in wood shop! I immediately ordered wood for my first project—a record cabinet on legs with sliding glass doors.

When my first project was finished, the wood shop teacher handed me my grade, a B+! To my surprise, he said that he was proud of me! Then he added, "Barb, when you first approached me about coming into my class, I thought that you were more interested in being with the boys than learning about woodwork."

I replied, "Oh no!" I turned and walked away, smiling ear to ear.

To build very many of the picnic tables, I knew I would need a lot of lumber. With no money to buy what I needed, I had to be highly creative. Soon it hit me—I will go to construction sites and pick up discarded lumber! After dark, with a flashlight in hand, I would dig through piles and dumpsters. I filled my trunk with scraps, mostly two-by-fours. After I gathered enough to build several tables, I bought redwood stain and nails from the local building supply store.

For three summers, with Ed's help, I assembled, stained, and sold seventy-five children's picnic tables! Many of my weekends were spent sitting at an intersection of a busy road, holding up a sign next to my tables. Initially, the income paid for the gas for my car; but eventually, it financed a much-needed vacation for my family in Northern Minnesota.

Although Ed and I seemed to make ends meet, it became evident that our financial struggles and setbacks would probably never end. "How could we go forward?" I questioned.

We desperately yearned for a solid life direction and a ray of hope; neither of which we seemed to find nor could anyone give it to us. Then one evening a "ray of hope" arrived with a knock on the door.

The old screen door on the Hamel House always banged with every tap. So when someone knocked, it caught our attention immediately. Ed walked over and opened the door. There stood a man with the biggest smile on his face. He introduced himself as "Pastor Dave." His countenance and kind, gentle words comforted us like a warm blanket. After a brief conversation, he invited us to visit his church. That next Sunday, despite the frustration of getting a family of five ready and into the car on time, we attended Pastor Dave's church and were deeply blessed. This was the beginning of our spiritual journey as a family.

Baby Christians are believers who are new in their faith. They are slowly grasping the knowledge of who God is in their life. Direction and purpose had not yet been understood. Ed and I were at that point, we were baby Christians. We were moving down the path God had already set before us but had not realized it. Before we understood it, life's distractions and difficulties had us traveling down into a deep dark valley.

CHAPTER NINE

IN THE VALLEY

WRITING THIS CHAPTER WAS BY far the hardest thing I had to do. Retrieving the memories once laid to rest was emotionally draining. In many parts, it was painstakingly difficult because at one point in my life, my heart was torn in two. But God, who is the healer of all things, favored permanent forgiveness and restored all relationships. I pray this chapter touches and gives insight to those who are treading where I have been.

I had not been dating Ed long when it came time to introduce him to Jeremy who was five years old at the time. They seemed to "hit it off" right away. One warm spring day, Ed, Jeremy, and I decided to take a walk to a park near where Jeremy and I lived. It felt good to be outside. Acting all silly, Ed soon became the leader with Jeremy and me copying him, laughing, mimicking what Ed was doing as we went along the sidewalk. They continued up the sidewalk as I followed along behind, watching. They ran around a tree, slapped a light pole, and then jumped over a puddle of water. I marveled at their enthusiasm and delighted in their playfulness. The time really encouraged me, shedding a ray of hope on a possible relationship. I was sure that not just anyone would be allowed into my and Jeremy's world. I ran to catch up with them.

It had now been a year since Ed and I had started dating, and we began to seriously talk about marriage. Then I became pregnant, so wedding plans moved into action. After the wedding, we moved into a townhome and hung a wedding plaque on the wall that said, "Home Sweet Home."

Jeremy continued to visit his dad and grandparents every other weekend. Then on a sunny spring day, our son Mike was born. With the demands of a newborn baby intertwined with the newness of our marriage, I felt as though I was treading in high water. By the end of the day, I was exhausted. Meanwhile, I could sense that something else was developing just below the surface of our marriage.

Shortly after Mike was born, I saw in Ed a bond of intimacy with Mike that did not exist with Jeremy. Ed was attentive to and absorbed with his new son. But Jeremy was always disciplined. Ed would angrily tell him to "Stop hovering over the baby," "Don't be so loud," "You are going to hurt him!"

Although this upset me, I did not say a word—at first. But during the next two years, I became less tolerant and began to express my anger. We fought often about fairness, discipline, and feelings. During those two years, our daughter Missy was born, and we had moved three times! By the time we moved into the Hamel House, things began to change within the walls of our "not so sweet" home. With no warning, no "how to" books providing clear guidelines to "blended family" living, we were heading down a deep dark valley of despair.

Before long, I surrounded Jeremy with my invisible fence—I will call it protection. Then I began to take on an intruder that entered "the fence," Ed. He would break through to discipline in a way I saw as unjustifiable. My guard was up, and my anger flared. Inside the fence was Jeremy, who was confused and did not know who to trust. Consequently, he began to protect his security—me—his mother! Herein lies the blended family crisis: miscommunication, negative feelings, and eventually serious turmoil that can rip a family apart. Then when I thought it could not get any worse, it did.

By the time Jeremy was eight years old, he began to share his feelings with his dad and grandparents. He then took their reactions and concerns upon himself and brought them back home. He began to emotionally separate himself from the family. Meanwhile, as the crisis continued to escalate, bitterness stirred inside me toward Jeremy because I was constantly forced to defend myself. After all, I am his mother, and I have failed to protect him. In turn, my anger was directed at Ed, which caused him to defend himself. Like a vicious cycle spiraling out of control, it began to affect our other children.

One evening, after Dan had brought Jeremy home from a weekend, Jeremy nervously announced, "I want to go live with my dad."

Ed quickly challenged him with, "Go ahead, and see where that gets you."

"No!" I cried in anger. "Ed, tell Jeremy that you love him!" I pleaded. Then to Jeremy, I cried, "Tell Ed you are sorry!"

It was futile. Neither of them would budge.

When summer vacation came, I reluctantly packed up Jeremy's things to move him to his dad's. It was an exceedingly difficult time for me with my emotions being ripped apart. Then four months later, I got a call from Jeremy, asking me to come get him. He wanted to come back home. Dan's alcohol addiction was too much for a young boy to bear. My heart broke for him. It seemed that overnight Jeremy was becoming a teenager, and then things became even more complicated at home.

One afternoon Ed and I were arguing about how Jeremy would be disciplined when he got home. Tension and disagreement escalated to anger. Past injustices were hurled back and forth. Exasperated, Ed turned and walked out of the house to his truck. I followed along behind, determined to get the last word in. Suddenly, without warning, Ed turned toward me and shoved me violently. I flew backward and tripped over a log on the ground. The next thing I knew I was in midair. I came down with a twisting motion, and there was a loud cracking sound! I knew instantly that my leg was broken. In a panic, Ed ran to the house to call his brother and wife who lived nearby. They were there in minutes and quickly laid me on a piece of plywood and lifted it into the back of our station wagon. With every bump in the road, the pain was so intense I nearly passed out. We arrived at the hospital, and I was rushed into X-ray. Several minutes later, the doctor came in and told us that the tibia and fibula had twisted and snapped like a piece of celery. They pumped me full of morphine to dull the incredible pain. But the pain and agony I felt in my heart was *far* worse. For two days, Ed sat near my hospital bed, overwhelmed with remorse at what he had done. He had never touched me angrily before, and I felt his grief.

When I was dismissed from the hospital, I moved into my parent's home. With a cast the whole length of my leg, I was pretty much helpless. Stranded on the couch, I had a lot of time to think. Ed called often, and we confirmed our love for each other. We agreed that things needed to change. Alone in my room, late one night, I thought about the love that I had for my husband and the love I had for my son. As a wife and mother, I felt like I was being torn in two. My pillow was wet with tears. Exhausted, I finally fell asleep.

Soon after, with the help of family and friends from church, I was able to return home. Our plan was to seek counseling right away, but that did not work out. Four months after celebrating the removal of my fourth and final cast, we were left with huge medical bills. With effort to pay them, counseling was put on hold. Ed worked long hours, and I picked up another house-cleaning job.

I had been cleaning house for John and Patty for almost a year when one day I shared my situation with her. She confessed that she had noticed I was tired, overwhelmed, and at times angry. After that we began to talk extensively every time I cleaned. She expressed her concern, not only for Jeremy, but also for our marriage and the other children and the effect it was having on them.

One day as I arrived to clean, Patty said she wanted to talk with me. We sat down, and with careful consideration, she said, "Barb, John and I discussed your situation, and we want to help you and your family. We want to open our home to Jeremy. He can live with us as long as you need—even permanently."

I was not surprised by that as John and Patty have two adopted children of their own. They also had a *big* heart! Ed and I were deeply grateful and humbled by their offer. We now had to determine what was important and what was not. In our hearts, Jeremy, our marriage, and our other children were most important. Pride and failure had to be swallowed. After talking with Jeremy *and* getting his approval, we accepted their offer. Dan and his parents were then told of our decision, much to their disapproval. With my consent, they were still allowed to have Jeremy every other weekend.

Jeremy soon settled into their home, attending the same school as before. He quickly adjusted and seemed happy. John was a great role model for him. Ed and I finally started to seek counseling.

Sadly, Dan was very unhappy with Jeremy's living arrangements and was constantly threatening John and Patty. After three months, it became clear that he would not stop until the situation changed, even though Jeremy made it clear he wanted to stay. For the safety of their home and family, a restraining order had to be served on Dan. Soon, despite all our good intentions, Jeremy was back living with us.

One day, weeks later, I received a phone call from Dan. Immediately, I could hear the despondency in his voice, and so I lowered my guard. Our conversation was intense yet intimate. He shared his feelings, regretting the turmoil he had put me through, during and after our marriage. Suddenly, to my shock and amazement, he asked for my forgiveness. Every part of me caved in. Compassion and forgiveness overwhelmed me. I knew the act of forgiveness was from God. I quickly responded "yes" and then asked, "Would you forgive me of all the times I wronged you?"

He answered, "Yes."

The conversation ended with Dan telling me that I was a good mom and Ed was a good guy.

"I love you," he said.

I did not know how to respond to that. He hung up the phone. I sat and stared out my living room window with an unsettling feeling. I thought about the conversation and how odd the exchange of sentiments was. I kept it to myself.

Three days later, one week before Jeremy's thirteenth birthday, Dan was killed in a motorcycle accident. Under the circumstances and in respect for Dan's family, we closed the door to the whole painful past and never opened it up again.

It was abundantly clear that Ed and I had to do something about our situation. It was now at a point of crisis. Despite all that had gone wrong, we still had a steadfast love for each other, and so we persisted in our willingness to heal. Our faith in God, who already knew our circumstances, accomplished the hardest part of our healing through forgiveness. Prayer was crucial. God then opened a door, which lead us on a new journey—moving to the South.

The challenges and heartaches that Ed and I faced throughout our first years of marriage brought awareness and compassion for families living in a blended family situation. For this reason, I am moved to elaborate more on the topic.

In a blended family—step-family—situation, one or both adults have been married before. In some cases, it involves a single-parent situation from a previous relationship. One or both has lost a spouse through death or divorce and have children from the previous marriage. They fall in love and decide to remarry and, in turn, create a new, blended family. Fortunately, many blended families work out their relationships and live together successfully, but unfortunately, many do not survive.

Our first mistake that comes to mind is that we did not get "knowledgeable" information *before* we got married, although there were few resources back then. However, today there is no excuse not to research material on the blended family. Resources are now abundant! Do not assume that your love will carry you through everything. The library has many books as well as bookstores, and I would recommend ones that are Christian-based. You can also Google blended families; you will be amazed at the amount of information you will find. I spoke with my pastor, and to my surprise, he had a whole folder of information and resources.

Before you make a commitment to get married, do your homework. Had we known then what we know now, we could have prevented so much stress and conflict. For those couples going into a marriage and feel that their blended family arrangement is not an issue, do not overestimate yourselves. One time Ed and I sat down with a couple who were planning to get married and shared our concerns for them. They were stepping into a blended-family relationship unprepared. We carefully asked them if they had done any research or talked to anyone about the "blended family." They quickly assured us they did not have any issues or doubts that it would not work. We ended that conversation, not wanting to intrude by telling them they were probably wrong. Ed and I hoped that they *were* right, but they were not. One year into their marriage, conflicts surfaced, and it was hard for us to watch.

As Ed and I treaded through the stepfamily crisis, we silently believed that we were failures, only to discover later that what we had experienced should have been expected; but we did not realize it! It is important to recognize that a blended family cannot and will not function in the same way that a traditional family does. It has its own special dynamics and behaviors. There are many possible combinations of blended relationships, in our case, stepfather and stepson. Each case and situation have its own unique elements. My emotions and misunderstandings got in the way when I first realized Ed's attention and love for "our" son was different from his love for Jeremy. It was different because his relationship between the two sons was different. I perceived it as Ed not loving Jeremy at all. What a horrible misconception! Division quickly developed between us. Again, had I recognized and understood the dynamics and behaviors of a blended family, I would have accepted Ed's love-relationship differences between our son and Jeremy. Also, Ed would have been more aware that he needed to be sensitive about not having the same love but showing equal love for the boys.

Another challenge we faced was discipline. This is the most common problem in a blended family. Lack of agreement on discipline can quickly disrupt family unity. I had no idea that Ed's disciplining Jeremy would turn into such an issue and how my emotions would play into it. In the very beginning of our marriage, we did not communicate to each other what disciplining would be like in our home. Parents should discuss the role each stepparent will play in raising their respective children. This will make the transition smoother. In talking with the child or children about rules ahead of time, they will know what to expect and what is expected of them. That will minimize confusion. Communication between all members of a family is critical, especially in a blended family.

When Jeremy wanted to go live with his dad, all he wanted was to feel safe, loved, and secure. Always remember that the child is the child, and the parent is the parent. Children want to know that their parents are in control—that is their security! It is the role of every parent—natural, adopted, or step—to know and accept their responsibility for raising children properly. Then hopefully, the children will respond by honoring their parents—birth or step.

Throughout the Bible, God instructs us how to care for our children and others as well. In Ephesians.4:29, it says, "Do not let any unwholesome talk come out of your mouths, but only what is helpful for building others up according to their needs, that it may benefit those who listen."

Ephesians 4:2 says, "Be completely humble and gentle; be patient, bearing with one another in love."

Ephesians 6:4 says, "Fathers, do not exasperate your children, instead bring them up in the training and instruction of the Lord."

In Matthew 18:10, Jesus says, "See that you do not look down on one of these little ones. For I tell you, that their angels in heaven always see the face of my Father in heaven."

We must have concern for all children as God has concern for them. Allow children to approach you. Take time to listen to them despite your busyness. Listening is priceless. God has put into your care His richest blessings and gifts—His children.

CHAPTER TEN

ASCENDING THE VALLEY AND HEADING SOUTH

THE GOOD THING ABOUT A valley as you walk through it, eventually, it ends. As we forged a pathway, striving to get out of the painful and difficult dark valley, we strained to see a light. Though we did not fully recognize the light, we were comforted that it was there. While reaching up and drawing closer to each other, for the first time, we encountered a group of people who came along side us. Pastor Dave talked about his "church family" when he paid us a visit. In time, this church family welcomed Ed, me, and our children, surrounding us with genuine love, encouragement, and prayer. We had our biological family, but this was different, and we began to understand its importance.

One day, during the Christmas season, after a church service, Ed, I, and the kids walked out to the parking lot to go home. When we got to our car, we found a big surprise—bags filled with groceries and presents marked with our names sat in the backseat. There was no note identifying the giver, just a card wishing us a Merry Christmas. We received the gift with thankfulness and wonder. While embracing our new church family, we were inspired to persevere in faith. Soon we felt as though we were shown stepping stones, which, in time, helped us out of the dark valley.

We had closed the door to our stepfamily crises and began to pray that God would guide us and heal the damage that we had caused. It was also clear that we needed to make improvements in our lifestyle. This forced Ed to decide to go to school to pursue a computer engineering degree. At first, we did not realize how much commitment, patience, and hard work it was going to take to get Ed through school and the sacrifices that would have to be made.

During the next year, Ed went to school, studied hard, and worked a job. I also picked up extra odd jobs while managing the household. The challenges were difficult, but the reward was enormous when Ed graduated. He was offered a job that was beyond his wildest dreams. Within three months, we had packed up and moved from the old Hamel House in Minnesota to Wisconsin. Shortly after arriving in Wisconsin, we packed up again and arrived in Atlanta, Georgia, where Ed started working for a large corporation. We did not know it at the time, but the change of events and location were going to quickly impact our lives.

Moving out of the Hamel house—heading down south

As soon as the kids were settled into school, I went to work as a hostess at a Cracker Barrel restaurant. Greeting and seating customers seemed easy, but when the first words came out of my mouth, I was pegged as a

"Northerner." With time, I picked up enough of a Southern drawl that my accent was not constantly being brought to my attention.

One evening, during the Christmas season, one of our neighbors invited Ed and I along to go look at "lots." Through his Southern drawl, I heard him say "lights." Excited to go, we jumped into the back seat of their car. I had always loved driving around taking in the Christmas "light" displays. I soon became frustrated as the car drove quickly past all the houses that were lit up. I wished he would slow down because we were missing all the Christmas sights. Soon we drove into a dimly lit cul-de-sac, and our neighbor stopped the car. Confused, I did not say a word. Then the lady pointed into a grassy knoll and said, "What do you guys think of that lot?"

It was then I noticed the "for sale" sign. Too embarrassed to say anything, I just nodded with disappointment.

Living away from Minnesota opened up the door to opportunities we would not have otherwise experienced. Although we missed our families and friends, Ed and I were given a chance to heal and enjoy a whole new life. Yet now Ed and Jeremy's relationship became reserved and predictable.

We started to attend a gospel-centered church, where God showed us a whole new way of church—Southern style. One Sunday morning, after the worship music ended, the pastor began with prayer. A hushed quiet covered the church as the pastor spoke. Suddenly, I could hear a slow but noticeable door squeak coming from the back. I turned around to see what it was. The door to the sanctuary was open, and there stood a stranger to everyone. He was a large man, and I could not help but notice the clothes he wore. Grease and dirt-stained, his ragged clothes hung on his body. Rope held up his pants. Duct tape held his sandals onto his grotesquely dirty feet. The greeter pointed the man to an empty seat—right next to my son, Mike! Surely he was not going to sit next to a boy that gagged at the slightest unpleasant odor! I quickly looked away, hoping the man would find a different empty chair.

After the pastor said "Amen," he looked up and was caught completely by surprise at the sight of the large unkempt stranger now standing in the aisle. Suddenly, the man began to speak. "I am sorry for coming in late, pastor, but I am part of the traveling carnival going on across the street. I noticed your church and … well, I thought I would attend."

The pastor instantly gave a big welcoming smile and told him to have a seat. Now, being so close, the odor coming from him was way beyond unpleasant! People began to cover their noses as inconspicuously as possible. The man looked at the empty chair next to Mike and quickly sat down. Mike turned to me with his eyes wide and a serious look on his face. I whispered into his ear, "The service will be over soon."

The pastor continued, when, to everyone's surprise, right in the middle of his message, the stranger stood up and apologized, saying, "I am sorry for interrupting, pastor, but I need to get back to work now, thank you for letting me come in."

The pastor smiled and replied, "No, thank you for coming today! Anytime the carnival comes to town, you come visit us."

"I will!" the man said with a smile and then walked out of the church.

There was no snickering or under-the-breath comments, insinuating a "how dare he." The pastor simply continued his message. To most sitting in the service that day, the situation was uneventful, but to me, this was a true testimony of God's genuine love and compassion shown through His people. My eyes were opened, and so was my heart.

In our neighborhood, thick with tall Georgia pines, red clay, and showy azaleas, was also a wonderful family. They were the Crumbleys! Dave, Lisa, and their two children were as Southern as cornbread in a hot iron skillet! One day, shortly after we had met, Ed and I went out to dinner with Dave and Lisa. We had just finished our meal when Dave stood up and motioned for us to move to the empty table next to the table we were at. Not knowing what to say, Ed and I stood, along with Lisa, who thought nothing of it. Curiosity churning, Ed soon asked why we moved. Dave said with a crafty grin, "Man, so we could have a clean table for our dessert!" Initiated into Dave's playful yet mischievous world, had Ed and I laughing from that moment on.

One weekend our two families went camping up in the Appalachian Mountains. The last evening at our campsite, it rained continually. Not able to enjoy the evening by the campfire, we called it a night. After the kids were settled into Dave's van for the night, Ed and I headed into our tent, and Dave and Lisa went to theirs. Suddenly, Lisa let out a holler, "Oh no! Our tent is sitting in water!"

Although their air mattresses saved their sleeping bags from getting wet, they could not stay in their tent. So like a good neighbor, we made room for them in ours. The rain began to pound, which had me hoping that the years of patching our old tent would keep the rain out. We lay snuggled in our sleeping bags, laughing as we shared stories. Then suddenly, I was hit by a drop of water and then another. I quickly set a cup to catch the now steady drips. Soon Lisa was hit by a drip and then another. Pots and pans were brought in from the outside. Before long, a little stream of water made its way through the inside of our tent. The sleeping bags were moved to the center, and as it poured outside, we encountered more drips inside. Needless to say it was a long night. If we had been with any other couple through this dilemma, it would have been disastrous. But with the Crumbleys, it was like being in a humorous comedy—we laughed hilariously all night.

The rain had subsided by early morning. Lisa and I got up and prepared a bacon-and-eggs breakfast. The men pulled the soaked contents out of the tents and packed up the vehicles so that after we ate, we could be ready to leave. Before leaving our muddy campsite, we laid our old and worn-out tent to rest. Both families stood like soldiers in a row, facing the campsite dumpster. Ed cupped his hands in front of his mouth and gave a trumpet sound. Dave walked ceremoniously past us, carrying our old tent, bound in a ball. Hoisting it over the side of the dumpster, he let go, and it hit the bottom with a thump! We all saluted and then jumped into the vehicles and headed out of the mountains and back to the comfort of our homes.

For the next two years, our friendship with the Crumbleys grew. I joined Lisa in her house-cleaning business, while Ed and Dave shared their passion for music. Our kids were inseparable. Lisa taught me how to cook Southern dishes, like skillet cornbread, collard greens, sausage balls, and her delicious Southern fried chicken. She also taught Ed how to make the best sweet iced tea. The first thing you did upon entering the Crumbley house was to go to the refrigerator and pour yourself a tall glass of cold sweet tea!

Realistically, Ed and I knew in the back of our minds that we probably would not live in the South permanently, so in the meantime, we wrapped ourselves in the life lessons that it brought us. We began to understand that God was leading in our lives. Instead of wondering about what is on the road ahead or worrying about what we should do if or when, we began to focus on Him. We were taking baby steps in the realm of faith. But other things were also going on in my heart. I continued to be pierced by low self-esteem, guilt, which now became a burden, and shame. Our time in the South had been like a bandage covering the things from my past. However, one day "shame" revealed itself again.

My day had been uneventful, so I decided to bake some cookies while the kids were at school. The aroma of fresh-baked cookies filled the house. As I pulled the last batch out of the oven, the phone rang. I threw the oven mitts onto the counter and picked up the phone. On the other end of the line was my mom. Her voice seemed strained and apprehensive. "What's wrong, Mom?" I asked.

She began to explain, "Barb, there's something in the Minneapolis paper you may want to know about."

Aware of the many old secrets in my life, I hesitantly asked, "What?"

"Before I say anything else, I must confess something that's difficult for me to say," she said and went on to explain with great emotion what my brother Rick had told her years ago about what my dad's friend, Bill, had done to me at his cabin.

My mind and body instantly cringed in shame, and I could barely speak. Mom struggled to talk. "I'm so sorry for what you had to go through," she said. "I regret not talking to you about it."

To ease her pain and quickly cover my shame, I told her, "Mom, it's been eighteen years since that happened, and I have put it away."

There was no way I could tell her about the effects that the experience had on my life. She then continued to tell me what she had read in the newspaper.

"Bill, a sixth-grade teacher, was charged with multiple counts of second-degree criminal sexual conduct, alleging that he had sexually touched girls in his classroom. In court, he denied it. Investigators learned that complaints were filed against him over the years. However, the school authorities were always unable to confirm any wrongdoing. Bill had posted bail and was freed. Police investigators working on the case had their hands tied and said, 'Allegations of inappropriate touching is difficult to prove.'"

Mom asked me if I wanted the phone number of the lieutenant who was in charge of the case. "Absolutely!" I said to her.

We finished talking and hung up the phone. My mind was racing as I sat down. As I began to reflect on that horrible night so many years ago, my anger surfaced.

The next morning I paced back and forth before finally picking up the phone to call the investigator. I did not know if I would be able to help or not, but I wanted to tell my story. Knowing that he was doing this to other girls angered me beyond words. The lieutenant answered the phone. I took a huge breath to calm my nerves, and then eighteen years of bottled-up shame and anger surfaced. I choked back the tears as I told him that I was calling from Atlanta, Georgia, and that my mom had told me about the case. Then I blurted out, "This man sexually assaulted me when I was fifteen."

He immediately stopped me and told me to stay on the line. He soon came back and told me that our conversation was being recorded and listened to by others in the police department. He said, "Okay, Barb, start from the beginning."

For the next twenty minutes, I cried, shook, and revealed every detail of what led up to and transpired during that night. I shared incidences that occurred during the year Bill was at our family farm. It all came out. When I finished, I was emotionally drained. The lieutenant thanked me for my statement and the courage it had taken to give it. He then asked for permission to use my statement in court. Without hesitation, I agreed.

Three weeks slipped by when the phone rang again, and it was the Minneapolis police. The lieutenant called to personally give me the news. Bill had been found guilty on numerous charges. Then he announced, "Bill will spend the rest of his life in prison."

He shared with me that this man had been bringing other young people up to the cabin for years.

Through all this, I found some degree of healing in my heart, but unforgiveness remained. But at least there was justice.

The three years in Georgia had raced by, when Ed was given the opportunity to work for IBM back in Minneapolis. We had to make a decision about moving back to Minnesota, and it came down to us missing our family and them missing us. It was time to go home.

After school let out for the summer, we were packed and ready to go. The last people to say goodbye and the hardest to say goodbye to were the Crumbleys. Hugs were shared and tears were shed as we said goodbye. Driving down the street, I turned to take one last look at our house nestled in the tall pines. We headed North—to home. Our time in Georgia was like dipping our hands into a clear, cool stream—we left refreshed.

CHAPTER ELEVEN

HOME AGAIN

EXCITEMENT GREW AS WE CROSSED the border into Minnesota. The sun felt warm on my face as I gazed out the window at the rows of corn emerging through the soil. Fields of alfalfa spread as far as the eye could see. In Georgia, tall pine trees and kudzu covered everything that stood in its way, lining the roads, making it hard to see. *The scenery in Minnesota certainly is different from Georgia*, I thought.

Meanwhile, Jeremy, now seventeen years old, kept a firm grip on the steering wheel as he drove with purpose. Mike and Missy rode with Ed in the big rental truck. We were almost there. Then three hours later, I heard Mike holler into the walkie-talkie, "I can see Grandma and Grandpa's house!"

As we turned to drive up the long gravel driveway, I was deluged with a flood of memories coming to mind. After long hours in the car, coming to a stop, we all jumped out and stretched. We were home.

Because we had not found a place to live yet, we rented a storage unit for our belongings. Mom and Dad agreed to let us stay with them until we found a place of our own. Later that afternoon, family and friends arrived at the farm to celebrate our homecoming. A potluck picnic was served, and the kids, thrilled to be back with their cousins, competed in a game of croquet.

By now, Ed and I were financially secure, so we decided to buy a parcel of land in a development to build our first home. During the next three months, we became overwhelmed with all the decisions that had to be made. Also, living with my parents was becoming stressful, not only for us, but for them as well. If that was not enough, besides building a house, Ed working a new job and commuting, settling three kids into three different schools, my new job and missing our home and friends in Georgia, I found myself pregnant.

Back to Minnesota from Georgia

I need to go back in time to when we lived in Georgia. While talking with a gynecologist one day, she suggested that if we were going to have any more children, now would be the time. I was thirty-five years old. Ed and I discussed this, and we agreed to have one more child. There were no plans of moving at that point, so we began the process. Knowing that I was "fertile myrtle," we expected I would become pregnant right away but to no avail. So when we found ourselves moving back to Minnesota, we decided to put it on hold or maybe even it would not happen at all!

It was evident that God wanted us back home during this time. I was five weeks along when I discovered I was pregnant. Ed and I wanted to tell our kids in a fun, surprising way, so we called them together at the table. They each were given four puzzle pieces then were told to work as a team to put the puzzle together. The completed puzzle would announce the news! When the last piece was put in place, Jeremy instantly smiled; Mike and Missy quickly caught on. With my parents by our side, we all cheered and celebrated.

It came time to share the news with our best friends, Tom and Coleen. One evening, as we gathered in their kitchen, Ed and I announced our big news. Unexpectedly, we were taken aback by the startled looks on their faces. Was it shock? Unbelief? I was quickly worried not only by their looks but also by their silence and asked, "What is wrong?"

Coleen burst out laughing and replied, "We were just going to announce 'our' news—I am pregnant!" What joy to share in such a time as this.

A few weeks later, while I was at work, I noticed that I was spotting. Then two hours later, mild cramps spread throughout my lower abdomen. Scared, I called Ed and then my doctor, who advised me to come to the clinic right away. After the exam, the doctor walked around to my side. With a sober look, he said, "I'm sorry, Barb, you've miscarried."

My heart broke, and I was numb. Because I was eight weeks along, he ordered a routine ultrasound to be sure that nothing else was going on. I could barely dress myself because of the news. The grief was overwhelming. I called Ed and told him the sad news and asked him to meet me at home. Choking back tears, I walked slowly over to the attached hospital for my ultrasound.

The chill in the room caused me to shiver, so the nurse laid a warm blanket over me. Soon the technician came in and asked me some brief questions. I lay quiet in my thoughts as she pulled the ultrasound probe over my abdomen. She suddenly stopped and gave me a look that concerned me. Standing up, she asked me to stay lying and said she would be right back. As soon as she left, I stretched my neck to look at the monitor but could not make sense of any of it. *What was it she had seen?* I wondered with alarm.

Several minutes later, the technician came back with two other doctors. They probed my belly and pointed at the monitor as they talked in doctor language among themselves. The technician finally turned to me and said in amazement, "You have another baby in you!"

I was speechless to say the least. She quickly showed me the little heartbeat and commented, "It is a good strong beat, and everything else looks good!"

I was so overwhelmed with emotion I barely remember getting dressed. On one hand, I grieved for the life that was lost, and on the other, I was ecstatic for the life that was inside me. I was thankful to be driving home alone, having much-needed time to myself.

Our newly built house could not have come any sooner. Excitement grew as the kids eagerly unpacked boxes in their rooms. I was relieved just to have the couch moved in so I could rest my new expanding belly. Ed was relieved to have the move behind us. That night, as I laid in bed, I could not help but chuckle as I pictured my parents running around the house, flailing their arms, hooting, and hollering, "Yippee, they are gone!"

"Freedom!"

Collen and I

Sorting through socks, organizing spices, even cleaning out the refrigerator were some of the things I did while in the early stages of labor with the other kids. The tugging feeling had not eased up all day. I was at my due date, so I expected that I was in the beginning of labor. I called Coleen to see if she felt any signs of labor. She had not. Ed came home early from work.

During the day, my contractions became more noticeable. By late evening, my bags were packed for the hospital, and the kids were packed for their stay at my parents. Missy, almost ten, kept track of the contractions. Concentrating on my breathing, I relaxed in a warm bath. "Okay!" I would yell out from the tub, alerting her of another contraction.

She would write it down and then report back on the interval. The warmth of the water felt good. I closed my eyes, reflecting on this memorable day. I am aware of coincidences, but I am also aware of miracles in life. It was March 28, my deceased brother Steve's birthday. I believe that God gave me the miracle of a baby, new life, on the anniversary of his birthday. After talking with my parents months earlier, if I had a boy, we would name him Steven.

Suddenly, I was jolted with another contraction. "Okay!" I shouted to Missy again.

She shouted back, "Mom, they are eight minutes apart!"

It was time to leave for the hospital. Although I knew, from experiences, I could be waiting all night, Ed was nervous and wanted to leave. First, we dropped Mike and Missy off at my parents. They would wait for our call letting them know when to bring the kids to the hospital so that they could be part of the birth.

Jeremy was on a trip with friends, so he was notified I was going to the hospital. As I had predicted, the night was long and uneventful. Then things changed. By early morning, Ed called my parents and said, "It's time."

Then he called Coleen, who was due to have her baby, and she was on her way. While the contractions intensified, we waited for Doctor Cady to arrive. Ed got the video camera ready. I fought not to push.

Suddenly, from around the corner, my parents walked in with the kids, and right behind them was Doctor Cady. He quickly instructed everyone to move into the room. My dad had never experienced a delivery before and began to get nervous. He had planned to be outside in the waiting room. But Doctor Cady, busy preparing for the delivery, blocked his escape route. Dad was called to the corner of the room where he stood frozen!

I was ordered to start pushing when Coleen ran into the room. With her bulging belly, she squeezed past the doctor and joined the others in the room. I pushed again and then again. "Get it out!" I hollered, and with one last push, out came a beautiful baby boy!

Filled with emotion, Ed bent down and said, "Welcome to the world, Steven."

I glanced over at my parents and saw tears streaming down their faces—it was a miracle.

"You get to come home with us today!" Missy said as she dressed her baby brother.

It was Easter Sunday. Ed helped me into the car. "Let's go home," he said with a smile.

Once again, we traveled down the road God had so lovingly set before us, and we felt blessed.

Jeremy holding Steven on graduation day

CHAPTER TWELVE

THE RIGHT WAY

SOMETIMES, WHILE DRIVING, YOU CAN come to a fork in the road, a place where you either veer to the left or right. One way is "wrong," and one way is "right," and you don't always have a lot of time to make a decision. One day Ed took a turn going the wrong way, but in the end, it was the right way.

It was a lazy Saturday morning when Steven climbed into our bed as our eyes opened to a bright spring day. His playfulness entertained us as we stretched and contemplated whether to get up. Then without much thought, I turned to Ed and said, "I need to go to Walmart today."

"Why?" he questioned as he yawned.

"I don't really know. I just need to go," I replied, almost questioning myself.

"Okay, I'll go with you," he said, adding, "I have to stop at a building supply store too."

We got up, showered, and dressed. Ed began to prepare his usual Saturday morning pancakes. I poured a cup of coffee, grabbed a piece of paper and a pen, and went into the living room where Mike and Missy sat watching cartoons. Sipping on the coffee, I tried to recall what it was that I needed at Walmart. I set the cup down and looked up, staring into space as if waiting for someone to tell me. Tapping the pen on the paper, I knew there was something!

Suddenly, Ed shouted from the kitchen, "Pancakes are ready!"

Maybe eating breakfast would help me remember. I laid the pen down and went to the kitchen.

Mike and Missy had no interest in going shopping, so I got Steven ready to go with us. As soon as Ed backed the car out of the garage, I hollered to the other kids that we were leaving. On my way out the door, I grabbed my shopping list then foolishly realizing I still had not written anything on it.

"I'll think about it on the way," I decided.

A few minutes later, I commented to Ed, "What a beautiful day."

He nodded in agreement as he turned onto the main road. Suddenly, it dawned on me that Ed had turned the wrong way! Walmart was the other direction! "You went the wrong way," I said, puzzled, as we had been there many times.

He quickly realized the mistake. But with cars already lined up behind us, we could not turn around. Then I remembered a new Walmart had just opened in the town next to us, the direction we were going. There was a building supply store nearby as well. With the confusion gone, we continued the "wrong" direction to the new Walmart. Once again, I sat looking at my blank shopping list, trying to remember what it was I needed.

The sun was glaring bright as we arrived at our destination and turned into the large parking lot. The sun now in his eyes, Ed instantly pulled the visor down so he could see where to drive. Squinting, I could see down the parking lot to where a young man was pushing shopping carts together. Then as we got closer, the young man stopped, turned around, and looked right at us. To our amazement, it was Jeremy! Because he had been living with his grandparents, Dan's parents, he had not had the opportunity to tell us about his new job. When he had applied, he was immediately hired and started work the same week. He was now a senior in high school and needed money to pay for his car.

Jeremy beamed ear to ear, waving, as we drove up to him. Ed rolled his window down, and I leaned over the console to talk my son. The guys chatted for a moment when Ed unexpectedly asked Jeremy if he wanted to go to lunch with us. *Didn't we just have breakfast?* I thought. This took me by surprise.

"Sure!" Jeremy replied with excitement. "Let me go tell my boss that I'm going to lunch."

Confused, I thought, *He's going to "tell" them he is going to lunch?* Didn't he just start the job, and now he is telling them when he is going out to lunch?

Before Ed could say another word, Jeremy took the carts and hurried into the store. Within moments, he came back out and jumped into the back seat with Steven. The two boys agreed on pizza before we got out of the parking lot. I was still stunned.

At the restaurant, Jeremy scooted into the booth next to Steven. Ed sat across him. As they ordered, I recalled that it was "I" who woke up this morning and mentioned going to Walmart. It was Ed that had taken the "wrong" turn. I was tempted to ask if they had planned this, but I knew in my heart they had not.

Jeremy told Ed about the new job and the car he had just bought. I wanted to join into the conversation, but before I got a word out, I felt as though I was silenced. Then it happened—like I had longed and hoped for so many years—Ed asked Jeremy three simple words: "How are you?"

It was a heartfelt question. To the people sitting around us, if they had been listening, it was words of casual conversation. But to me, it was immense. I busied myself with Steven, keeping my thoughts silent. Ed and Jeremy talked about work, school, plans, and cars over pizza. Pretending to enjoy the lunch, because I was not the least bit hungry, I thought about the morning. It was clear that only God could have orchestrated the circumstances that led up to this point. He had set into motion the desire of His heart and mine. My desire to go to Walmart with a blank shopping list and Ed taking the "wrong" turn that ended up being the "right" way was His plan! We just did not know it at the time.

After we finished our lunch, Ed drove Jeremy back to work. He quickly thanked us for lunch and ran into the store. Driving out of the parking lot, it occurred to me that we had not even gone into the store. But I knew that I had already gotten what I needed.

CHAPTER THIRTEEN

STANDING IN THE CROSSWINDS

LIKE CROSSWINDS COMING FROM ALL directions, the next decade brought significant changes. Some were welcomed and celebrated, others were unexpected, while some were feared like a mighty storm approaching.

Gazing at myself in the mirror one day, I came to the realization that my appearance was changing. I had to accept the fact that a mirror cannot lie—I was aging. Ed was also showing signs as his head of hair, once the color of rich chocolate, was turning into salt and pepper grays. But the telltale sign of our time is through our children.

Jeremy finished high school and then moved to Chicago where he graduated from North Park College. He then traveled worldwide, settling in Saudi Arabia, where he worked for a large corporation for five years. After moving back to the States, he settled, married Breonna, and now has two children. He had grown up to be a wonderful man. Mike finished high school then graduated from trade school. At seventeen, he dated his high school sweetheart, Miranda. They were married eight years later. After his son and daughter was born, Mike was cured of his gag reflex with unpleasant odors! Our daughter Missy became a phlebotomist and has blessed us with two handsome grandsons.

We have always teased our youngest son, Steven, that he cannot marry, or move away for that matter, because he is such a joy to have around. (Although our grocery bill would decrease if he did!) Steven was well liked by those who knew him in school. However, school was a struggle for him. Ed and I continuously encouraged him, helping him set goals. Sometimes, with so many other things going on in our lives, it took a huge amount of patience to help him get through school.

When Steven was six years old, Ed and I noticed that he was constantly pulling at the neck of his shirt. By the end of the day, his shirt was usually stretched out of shape. At first, this was funny, and we would tease, "There he goes again, pulling at his shirt."

Then it became more frequent, almost obsessive. Two years later, it was obvious that movements on his face and body began to develop. We became concerned, as did his teachers, because his school progress was being affected. We set up an appointment with a neurologist to have Steven evaluated. At age nine, Steven was diagnosed with mild Tourette's Syndrome (TS).

TS is a neurological disorder characterized by repeated and involuntary body movements and uncontrollable vocal sounds called tics. They are not intentional or purposeful. The average onset of TS begins between the ages of seven and ten. Steven probably started at age six when we first noticed the shirt pulling.

TS occurs in people from all ethnic groups with males affected about three to four times more often than females. It is estimated that two hundred thousand Americans have the most severe form of TS, and as many as one in one hundred exhibit mild and less complex symptoms. Steven fell into this category. Although TS can be a chronic condition with symptoms lasting a lifetime, most people with the condition experience their worst symptoms in their early teens, with improvement occurring in the late teens and continuing into adulthood.

Steven's condition progressed as he became a teenager. It was amazing, in his case, how his tics would move from one arm and shoulder to the other, from one part of his face and neck to another. Almost weekly, it would shift into different body movements, sometimes even into his chest.

Steven was truly fortunate not to experience any teasing from other kids. His friends recognized and accepted his condition. However, school was a challenge as the TS seemed to interfere with his classes. He also struggled with the ability to complete his schoolwork. With the help of the school, he was assessed, and it was determined that he would take part in a special education program to help meet his needs. This helped him tremendously. (Thanks goes out to Ms. Mitchel!)

Tics are classified as either simple or complex. Simple motor tics are sudden, brief repetitive movements that involve a limited number of muscle groups. Complex tics are distinct, coordinated patterns of movements involving several muscle groups. Although the symptoms of TS are involuntary, some people can sometimes suppress or camouflage their tics in effort to minimize their impact on functioning. However, people with TS often report a substantial build up in tension while suppressing their tics to the point where they feel that the tic must be expressed. Steven's teachers eventually understood that his getting up from his desk many times to sharpen his pencil was his way of expressing his tic.

Because school was difficult for Steven, summers were a welcome relief for him and for me as well. Baseball filled the summer calendar. His love and dedication for the game led to opportunities for him to play on a traveling team. Tics are often worse with excitement and anxiety but better during calm and focused activities. With Steven's calm, easy-going personality and his ability to stay focused during a game, his tics were rarely noticeable.

Ed and I have great memories of watching Steven, along with his teammates, compete in state, regional, and national levels for twelve years. By the time he was eighteen, his Tourette's had subsided. However, he will have to cope with it into his adult life, but he has learned to accept and manage this way of life. As to date, Steven is married to Allie, he has a son, and they have two more boys. I am happy to say our grocery bill has now decreased!

Just as our children became busy in their lives, so it did with Ed and me. Ed had started playing guitar when he was seven. His gift of and passion for music has richly blessed our lives and the lives of others throughout the years. He has had the opportunity to play in numerous secular and Christian bands, and he continues to play and lead worship ministries. On one occasion, we had an entire band set up in the Hamel House, with lights and all, to practice before a gig. There have been many nights when I have fallen asleep to Ed playing everything from "Stairway to Heaven" to "Amazing Grace." Thankfully, I understand the relationship he has with his five guitars, so there is no need for jealousy on my part.

Like Ed's passion for music, I have a passion for cooking and baking. When I was nine, to my parents' surprise, I ordered an Easy Bake Oven from a JCPenny catalog. I created cakes and cookies beyond what the instructions gave. In a selfish, self-satisfied way, I would relish in the fact that my brothers would fight over my little desserts as I proudly watched. Along with my love for cooking and baking came my love for cleaning houses. I know that may sound strange because not many people love to do that. But I grew up in a clean house. I recall many times coming home from school to the strong odor of bleach. Mom cleaned everything with it, saying it killed germs. I thought it did more damage than anything. Our sheets and towels were always blotted with white bleach spots.

I too love a clean house. Then I went on to clean other people's houses, and guess what? I even got paid! There were also perks! One time I retrieved a coffee maker out of a garbage can, fixed the electrical cord on it, and then used it for three more years. I have received used clothing, cookware, and plants that were almost dead. I also never had to order magazines as one of my cleaning customers provided enough of them to last me for years! Though I had good experiences with cleaning other people's homes, occasionally, I would find myself in trouble, like the time I arrived to clean a house to find a note of appreciation for my work. It had a vase of fresh-cut flowers sitting on it. *How nice of them*, I thought. That evening I received a phone call from the people, wondering if I had seen a bouquet of flowers that was for someone in the hospital. Oops.

Another time, after a couple left for work, I came to clean their brand new home. As I backed myself out of the master bathroom, washing the floor, I turned and set my pail of cleaning supplies onto the new plush carpeting behind me. Finishing, I picked up the pail that somehow tipped over and went to clean another bathroom. Later I returned to vacuum the master bedroom. Moving the vacuum cleaner back and forth, I quickly noticed a spot on the rug. I went over it again, and suddenly, it occurred to me that the spot was getting bigger! I got down on my knees for a closer look. I realized to my horror that the carpeting was disintegrating right before my eyes! The bottle of toilet bowl cleaner that had tipped over instantly came to mind. I began to frantically run around the spot as if somehow it would disappear. I reached down and pulled up handfuls of carpet and padding, exposing the subfloor beneath. I had to call the lady of the house. Reluctantly, I picked up the phone to call her.

"Hello, this is Sandy ... Hello?" I heard from the other end.

Before I could say one word, I lost it. Stumbling to get words out, I said "I'm sorry" over and over. Finally, Sandy stopped me and asked if I had broken the glass on the new coffee table. I said, "No."

"Then nothing else matters," she said in a calm voice.

Soon the carpet was repaired, and I was comforted by their kind words of appreciation.

While living down in Georgia, I joined my friend Lisa cleaning houses. One day, while cleaning a house for the first time, we noticed hundreds of black specks on our shoes, socks, and legs. With a closer look, we discovered that they were fleas! We ran out of the house, jumping and hollering, as the neighbor next door watched in astonishment.

Another time, after arrangements were made to clean a client's house while she was away on business and the man of the house would "supposedly" be gone to work, we arrived ready to clean. After unlocking the door, we entered the massive home. Suddenly, while standing in the foyer, we thought we heard voices coming from the upstairs. Though we were told that no one would be home, we stopped to listen. The house was quiet. Still uncertain, we slowly and quietly made our way up the stairs with our buckets of cleaning supplies and a vacuum cleaner. We came to a bedroom doorway and peered inside. We were shocked and bewildered by the unexpected situation we were witnessing. Then there was panic under the sheets! Suddenly, like two clowns in a circus performance, Lisa and I turned, crashing into each other while the buckets, mop, and vacuum went flying. Scrambling to gather them up, we nearly tumbled down the stairs. We bolted out the front door. Gasping for breath, we threw everything into the back trunk, jumped into the car and sped down the driveway. Not far down the road, we had to pull over for we could not see because of the tears running down our faces from laughing hysterically.

Evidently, the lady of the house resolved the suspicions because two weeks later, when we returned to clean, there was no sign of a man living in the house!

Because I came highly recommended, I would sometimes be hired over the phone and a key would be left for me to get into a house, even though the owners had never actually met me, and I would never meet them. That was the case with one of the client's I worked for.

Steven was only three and came with me once a month while I cleaned. For two years, we had a routine. Upon entering the house, we would be greeted by the couple's friendly little "Scottie" dog. I would slip a DVD in the player for Steven to watch, and he would snuggle with his blanket on the couch. I would get a stick of beef jerky from the snack jar in the kitchen for him. Then I would proceed to clean.

One day, as Steven and I arrived at the house to clean, the owner was just getting ready to leave. We talked briefly, and then she casually mentioned, "If you want, you can give the dog a treat each time you come."

I thought Steven would have fun doing that, so I asked, "Where are the treats?"

I gasped when she pointed to the jar on the counter. I was too embarrassed to tell her I had been giving them to Steven for two years!

In time, my house cleaning came to an end. I was very ready. I began to grow in experience with catering. Quite often, I would be asked to cater for family and friends celebrations or a church event. The door of possibilities was opening. Before long, my friend Kathy and I teamed up to see if there was any potential of starting our own business. This was the beginning of "Celebrations Catering."

Then like a mighty storm that roared in out of nowhere, it was September 11, 2001. The event shook our country, and hardships struck our church and our family. Although the country pulled together after the tragedy, the devastation left in its wake was staggering. Then the war with Iraq followed, and what had been our peaceful lives were forever altered. These tragic events unraveled many emotions and heightened the awareness of uncertainty and shook the illusion of security. We became worried over Jeremy's safety as he was still living in Saudi Arabia.

Near the end of the twentieth century, an endless flow of unexpected circumstances began to emerge. Ed lost his job of ten years and was not having any success in finding another one in his field of experience— computer engineering. At the same time, industry, in general, was severely depressed, and there was a hiring freeze in most companies. Businesses began to downsize, and more people were laid off. Many companies around the country and in Minnesota were closing their doors forever.

The doors were also being closed at the new start-up church we were attending and serving. Though thankful for the many people we had come to know, it was a heartbreaking decision, and we were all discouraged by the event.

Also, during this time, close friends of ours were going through a divorce. After twenty years of marriage, they closed the door and went their separate ways. It was hard to accept.

The storm slowly passed over, leaving me barely able to stand on my own feet. I began to feel hopelessness, not only with the world, but also with my life. Unknown to me, that would all change in a moment's time.

CHAPTER FOURTEEN

A NEAR ACCIDENT— OR WAS IT?

IT WAS A WARM OVERCAST day in August, and I was out and about, running errands. I had just come from Steven's school conference that morning and had left feeling disheartened. I also received a phone call that morning from a client who let me know they would not need my catering service. I had been depending on the job to help pay bills since Ed was out of work—I was discouraged. A little later, Ed informed me that the part-time job he interviewed for was filled. My mind was absorbed with worry. I finished up my errands and started the drive home. As I gazed at the road ahead of me, I thought, *Why do I worry about so many things I have no control over?* A blanket of sadness covered me, and it felt like the weight of the world settled on my shoulders.

In a moment's time, I decided that I did not want to go home. I just wanted to keep driving and not come back! Staring at the road ahead, I contemplated where I should go to escape my dread. The heavy, overcast sky, combined with the events of the day, made me tired. I looked up and said, "Lord, I don't want to go any further, not even one more mile."

As I refocused on the road, I saw a car barreling toward me. It was out of control! Holding tightly to the steering wheel, I slammed my foot on the brake, bracing myself for a head-on collision! Suddenly, I could hear loud screeching. In what seemed like a slow-motion, the car heading directly at me slid sideways, spun into the ditch, and came back up onto the road, missing my car by inches!

Like a scene out of an action movie, dust and dirt whirled around me while I sat helpless at a dead stop, still gripping the steering wheel. As the dust billowed, obscuring my sight, I waited for the air to clear. Then sitting yards away from me, I could see the other car. The driver was staring at me while I sat frozen in my seat. Surprisingly, he smiled and waved at me. Then to my utter amazement, he simply drove off!

The thought "Did this 'really' just happen?" flashed through my mind. Still sitting in the middle of the road, with no other car in sight, I struggled to get my bearings and start moving again. Suddenly, something awakened in me—I realized just how close I came to my life dramatically changing in a moment's time. Tears rolled down my cheeks. The drive home gave me the time to gather my thoughts and ask the Lord to forgive me for my distrusting heart.

Pulling into the driveway, I saw Steven standing there, tossing a baseball up into the air. To him, it was just an ordinary, uneventful day. The sight brought a smile to my face. I jumped out from the car and gave him a giant and probably embarrassing hug. He did not question or pull away from my sudden odd behavior. I was home and so thankful for that.

Even as I recall that moment when my life flashed before me, I remember myself as someone who had slid into the depths of despair, having become sidetracked by weariness. I had lost my focus—keeping my eyes on the Lord. God so effectively reminded me that if I take my eyes off Him, I will crash under the weight of worries and cares. But if I focus on Him—always ahead of me, always with me—He already holds what is there and keeps me safe.

"Even youths grow tired and weary, and young men stumble and fall; but those who hope in the Lord will renew their strength. They will soar on wings like eagles; they will run and not grow weary; they will walk and not be faint" (Isa 40:30–31).

My weariness gave way to new strength as I began to trust and once again put my hope in my Heavenly Father. However, I had not yet discovered what God was capable of. But I would soon find out.

CHAPTER FIFTEEN

THE BATTLE IN MY CAR

IF I COULD DESCRIBE MY life at this point, it would be like holding a plate and filling it so full of food that a cherry tomato would not be able to stay on top—it would roll off! With my life being busy and my plate being full, finding time for anything else would be a challenge. But God had a plan to fit one more thing into my busy schedule—Himself.

I understood that God has a plan for each person who believes. But I was uncertain as to how that all played out for me, and besides, I felt unworthy of his provision. That uncertainty pushed me into being busy with church life and trying to become a good Christian woman. I felt, if I did things and tried to be good, He would certainly bring about His plan for me. What I was unaware of was that my relationship with Him was not growing.

One day my friend Marcy, who devotes much of her time teaching Bible studies, invited me to a study she was going to start leading in the fall. The study was called "Experiencing God" by Henry Blackaby. With my plate still full of doing things and lacking time and energy, I did not think I could commit to that. I told her I would consider it and get back to her. I never did. Weeks later, she called and asked if she should order my study guide. Although I still was not sure if I was able to commit to the time, I reluctantly said yes.

Weeks passed, and it was the night of Marcy's Bible study. I had just gotten home from a busy and stressful day. I was going to make a simple supper of soup and bread. Reaching for a saucepan in the cupboard, I noticed the study guide sitting on the counter. Suddenly, my head and shoulders dropped as if to say, "I really don't want to go tonight."

Opening the refrigerator, I was glad to see a leftover rotisserie chicken. While deboning what was left, I contemplated going.

I'm so tired, I thought. *Maybe I should just stay home. Besides, it's just the first night.*

Then I tried to come up with more excuses. As I finished preparing the soup, I looked over at the clock, which seemed to be staring back at me. With time running out, I finally gave in and decided to go.

I quickly swallowed the last spoonful of soup, threw on my sweater, and grabbed my study guide and purse. As I left out the door, I hollered goodbye to Ed and Steven who were still eating their supper. Ed hollered back, "Have fun!"

The church where Marcy was holding the Bible study was only seven minutes away. But what happened next made it seem *seven hours* away!

Driving down the road, I looked at the time. I realized I was running a little late. *I can't arrive late*, I thought as I lifted my foot off the gas pedal. "Besides, there's always next week, and then I can go earlier," I reminded myself. Then as if there were two of me in the car, I began to argue, "No, I need to go! Besides, I do not want to disappoint Marcy." Meanwhile, the car was slowing down and speeding up, depending on which of me was saying what. "This is crazy—just go home." I abruptly turned the car around and went home.

Walking into the house, I saw Ed and Steven were still at the table, talking. Setting my purse and study guide down, I took off my sweater and voiced aloud, "Don't even ask."

I marched past them and into the living room. Agitated over my decision to come home, I questioned myself, "What is happening?"

Then like a switch was thrown, I had the strongest desire to be at that study. So once again, I put my sweater on, grabbed my purse and study guide, and walked past Ed and Steven who were now waiting to see what I might do next.

Finally arriving at the church, I ran my fingers through my hair and checked my makeup so not to appear disheveled. The ladies were chatting and helping themselves to refreshments when I walked in. Marcy, standing across the room, saw me and smiled. We soon settled into our chairs to begin the study. Marcy opened in prayer. She thanked the Lord for bringing each of us to the study. I chuckled to myself. *He had to drag me!*

She continued to make clear that God desires each of us to experience Him to the fullest. It was in His plan for each of us to be there that night. My heart leaped and emotion filled me. "Thank you, my Lord," I whispered.

Little did I know that night the impact that the study would have in my life during the next year. The battle in my car, I believe, came from the enemy who frantically tried to hinder me from going. God knew it; that is why I had to be there that night.

CHAPTER SIXTEEN

THE DOOR THAT OPENED UP TO MY KITCHEN

I GOT OUT OF THE car slowly and stretched. Ed and I had just returned home from a weekend up by Lake Superior. We were feeling refreshed and energized from the relaxing getaway. This could not have come at a better time because, unknown to us, the next four years were going to be enormous!

After unpacking the car, I grabbed the stack of mail piled on the kitchen counter and went to sit down. Walking past the phone, I decided to check my voicemail first. Sure enough, there were messages, and one of them was going to change my life. "Barb, I know you have been looking for a catering kitchen for a while. Just wanted you to know there is a coffee shop that is going up for sale," my friend said excitedly.

I had been searching for a catering kitchen of my own for quite some time, so the news grabbed my attention. As I sat down with the mail, I decided I would check into it the next day.

Before I continue with my story, I need to explain what events had led up to this time.

Kathy, my catering partner, and I had catered together throughout the last few years. She then went on to be a head cook at a private school, using the school's kitchen as her licensed catering kitchen. I would help her often and wished that I could have the same kind of setup. But an opportunity like this does not happen very often—if at all! I know this because I had been searching for three years. During that search, I had gone through stages of giving up; to determination in finding anything to cater out of. I needed a licensed kitchen to cater to the extent that I wanted. Along with searching for a kitchen, I started attending the Bible study my friend Marcy was teaching. Little did I know that Bible study and how I got my catering kitchen would parallel each other in a miraculous way.

Now back to the story.

I decided not to call the coffee shop that was for sale, but instead, I would go there. I had never been inside and was curious as to what it looked like. As I entered, I could feel the warmth and coziness of the place. I ordered a cappuccino and sat down to observe what was going on. Lori, the owner, was not in, so I finished my drink and decided to come back the next day.

The next morning I returned and sat down with Lori. She shared about her situation and her difficult decision to sell. My heart ached for her as she had worked so hard to keep the business going. I left feeling sad for her but was impressed by what I saw in the coffee shop—a kitchen to cater out of.

That night, at the "Experiencing God" Bible study, Marcy led us through the unit called "Looking to God." The summary was to know and do the will of God. We learned that we are to deny self, self-centeredness, and return to a God-centered life. We must focus our life on God's purpose for us—not our own plans. God wants us to wait until He shows us what He is about to do through us. This was a huge revelation for me because

I began my catering journey thinking it was all about what "I" wanted, never thinking about where God wanted me.

Days after I had met with Lori, my son, Jeremy, now living back in the States after years in Saudi Arabia, sat with me to discuss the coffee shop. Jeremy has a business degree and was interested in partnering with me in the business. After discussing our options, he went to talk with a financial advisor. In the meantime, I researched the coffee shop business.

One day Ed and I sat down with Lori to discuss the business, and to our delight, she shared her Christian faith. A friendship soon blossomed between us.

The following week at Bible study, we studied the unit called "God Pursues a Love Relationship." The summary was to be loved by God is the highest relationship, achievement, and position in life. God created me and you for a love relationship with Him. When you have this relationship, He reveals more and more of Himself to you. This allows you to know "His plan" for you. I drove home from the study that night, yearning for a love such as that. I prayed that God would help me rid the junk that held my heart so that I could embrace His love.

The night was cold as I sat alone in my car in the parking lot across the street from the coffee shop. The solitude in the car allowed me to sort through my feelings. I gazed at the little shop that seemed to illuminate a warm glow into the dark. Inside, I could see Lori busy serving her customers. As I watched, I prayed. "Lord, where do you want me in all of this?" I asked with uncertainty.

I prayed for Lori and thanked Him for her friendship. As I continued to sit and observe, an overwhelming sense of peace and love wrapped itself around me.

During the process of exploring the possibilities of partnering with my son in the coffee shop, Jeremy was also interviewing with a company for a job in his field of work. I continued to research and visit coffee shops in other towns.

Excitement and anticipation grew all day as I looked forward to the evening Bible study. Each week the ladies in the group would ask how things were progressing with the coffee shop. It was fun to share with them how I sensed God's leading during the process. But I admitted to them I had a strange feeling that God had another plan for me.

That night, we studied the unit called "Love and God's Invitation." The summary was God is at work in the world, and He invites us to join him in that work. As I began to grasp what the lesson was saying, I considered what work would God have in mind for me. Will I know when and where? My mind wandered as Marcy prayed at the end of the study. Then on my way home, I thought about God's love for me and wondered how He would reveal His plan for my life. First, He had to take the initiative to open my "spiritual eyes" so that I could take in what He was about to do. "Lord, open my eyes that I may see and know your will," I asked prayerfully.

It had been a month since the phone call about the coffee shop. Jeremy and I needed to decide what we were going to do, and Lori needed an answer. This was a huge decision! Jeremy had not heard from the company he had interviewed with, and I was anxious to get a catering kitchen open. We agreed that I would call Lori in the morning with an offer.

Because my week had been so crazy, I did not have a chance to read my study guide in preparation for that night's Bible study. Marcy had us turn to the unit called "The Crisis of Belief," the turning point in following God's will. To my amazement the word "crises" comes from the word—are you ready?—"decision." The "crises of belief" is a turning point where you must make a decision. To me, this was another extraordinary revelation! How you respond at this turning point will determine whether you go on to be involved with God, in something God-sized, which only He can do, or you continue to go your own way and miss what God purposed for your life. The summary: Faith is believing in what God can do. Faith is confidence that what God has promised or said *will* come to pass.

After the study, I sat in my car and thought about what Marcy had said about the mustard seed and our faith in God. She had brought a mustard seed to show us just how tiny they are. With only a mustard seed-sized faith in God, nothing is impossible. The thought really impacted me in a profound way, and I prayed, "Lord, I want to have faith the size of a mustard seed."

I believed God already knew exactly where He wanted me in my catering journey. That night I truly put my trust in Him.

The next morning, as I prepared to call Lori to make an offer, the phone rang. It was a parent from a charter school, informing me that their school was in desperate need of a caterer to bring in lunches. Disappointed to lose such an opportunity, I had to tell her that I did not have a licensed kitchen. I wished her luck and hung up. I paused for a moment and was about to call Lori when the phone rang again! It was a friend calling to tell me that another coffee shop was closing its doors. Concerned, she said, "Barb, you need to think twice about buying a coffee shop!"

After she hung up, I stood by the phone, trying to comprehend what was happening. With Lori's coffee shop closing and now this one, I pleaded, "Lord, show me what to do— where do you want me?"

Then it was as if someone took me by the hand, put my jacket on me and my keys in my hand. I found myself in the car and on my way to the nearby town where the other coffee shop was closing. I had to know why they were closing! And I had to know now!

Pulling up to the curb in front of the coffee shop, I quickly noticed a sign posted on the front door. It said, "SORRY, BUSINESS IS CLOSED."

I walked up to the door and looked in—it was dark inside. *This can't be!* I thought as I went over to the front window to look in.

Cupping my hands to the glass so I could see inside, I noticed a silhouette of someone standing there. I quickly waved my hands to get their attention. A woman turned toward me and pointed to the sign on the door. I waved again and then knocked on the window.

"I have a question!" I hollered, hoping she could hear me.

She motioned for me to go away. I am sure she thought that I was someone determined to get a cup of coffee! Knowing that I was losing her attention, I took my finger and frantically wrote on the fogged window, a backward "? 4 U!"

Later I thought about this and realized it was God directing me because I would have never thought to do such a thing, especially so quickly.

The woman and I walked to the door. Cautiously, she slowly opened it up. I immediately smiled, hoping she could see that I was sane. Letting her guard down, she invited me in. I shared my situation with the coffee shop. Then as she shared her story, I began to feel discouraged. I wondered if this was my answer to buying a coffee shop. Then what happened next only God could have orchestrated.

Emotionally drained, the woman stopped talking and wished me the best. "I'm sorry this happened to you," I said as I turned and started to walk out.

Suddenly, she spoke up. "Oh, if you know anyone who would be interested, I also have a brand new catering kitchen just across the street. The lease and business are for sale!"

I quickly whirled around, feeling my heart trying to pound its way out of my chest. I asked as calmly as I could, "What … do … you … mean?"

The woman casually gave me the details. Meanwhile, standing there, I felt as though angels were holding on to me so I would not fall.

"How much are you asking?" I questioned her, trying to keep my composure.

She told me, and I knew I could afford it. I immediately wrote my name and number down and gave her the piece of paper.

"Please do not offer the catering business to anyone else. I'll call you back this evening," I begged as I headed back to the door.

Then to my utmost surprise, she added, "Oh, by the way, there is a charter school we are contracted with, and they are in immediate need of a caterer. You'd have that as well, if you're interested."

That had been the first phone call that I had received this morning, turning down the offer! I was ecstatic!

That night Ed, my friend Kathy, and I went to inspect the catering kitchen. I knew instantly it was perfect. Then as if God wanted to confirm my thoughts, my phone rang, and it was Jeremy. "Mom, did you call Lori today?"

"Not yet," I replied.

Then he announced, "I received an offer from the company I interviewed with—I can't pass it up."

Unimaginable confirmation!

The next morning I could not procrastinate any longer. I called Lori to tell her about my change of plans. As I shared the details, her initial response was disappointment and surprise. However, she assured me that I was doing the right thing. Then her next words were additional confirmation. "Honestly, Barb, I was beginning to feel that buying the coffee shop wasn't a good plan for you."

Excitement, combined with stress, filled the days ahead. Each step in the process of opening my business was difficult as I was learning "on the fly." After finalizing all the legal papers, lease contracts, insurance policies, state licensing, and city permits, I was exhausted and overwhelmed. But with each step, each bend in the road, and each mountain climbed, when I thought I could not make it over the next obstacle, I spoke to the Heavenly Father. His promise to be with me gave me the strength to persevere. Then there was one final hurdle to get over—the state Department of Health.

The Department of Health had to inspect my kitchen so that I could open for business the following day. The school needed lunches that Monday. I waited anxiously at my kitchen, peeking out the window every so often for the inspector who was to arrive soon. When I answered the door, and he walked in, I tried hiding my nervousness. He instantly got to work as I stood off to the side. He slowly moved about, opening doors, bending over to get a better look; then on his hands and knees, he looked under things. Every time he stopped and wrote on his clipboard, my heart would sink. Finally, he came full circle back to me. By this time, my hands were twisted and sweaty, and I could hardly take the pressure. He tore the sheet off the pad and handed it to me.

"Congratulations! You passed!" he announced, smiling.

I held my composure as I signed some papers and then walked him to the door. As soon as the door shut, a bubbling song of joy burst from within me. I cheered and jumped with exultation. Standing in the middle of the kitchen—my kitchen—I was filled and overcome with gratefulness.

Humbly, I said, "Thank you, Heavenly Father."

AUTHOR'S NOTE

THIS LAST CHAPTER WAS THE most difficult for me to write. Not because I made it complicated, but because the circumstances that took place during that time were so incredibly amazing. I still have a hard time wrapping my mind around it, let alone tell about it! No matter how I look at it, God had His hand on it.

One might ask, "How do you know it was God?"

God always has a way of working things out for our good because, first, He is good and, second, His will for our life is most always good. However, we must trust Him to do the right thing in the right way at the right time. He always has our best interest in mind. If not for this, one could think that this chapter was a large series of incredible coincidences.

Knowing God does not come through a program or method. It is a relationship with a person. It is an intimate love relationship with God. My time spent seeking and talking with my Heavenly Father during my "coffee shop journey" allowed me to grow in my relationship with Him. Through this relationship, God revealed His will and invited me to join Him where He was already at work. God accomplished through me something only He could do. My catering kitchen was His plan! He put me there!

Part two of this book holds the testimonies of God's work in my life. Each of the following chapters tells a story unique at the time. They consist of life lessons, people that impacted my life, blessings, and stories I am positive that even God was laughing.

PART TWO

CHAPTER SEVENTEEN

COULD YOU HOLD, PLEASE?

DURING ONE OF MY DIFFICULT years of trying to find my "niche" in life, I got a call from my cousin, Jackie. She is one of the most creative people with crafts that I know. Along with the many amazing projects she has accomplished, knitting was, by far, her most valued gift. Because of it, she was in demand for her knitwear. At one point, she bought a knitting machine that could knit a 180-row stitch in thirty seconds. Now I do not know much about knitting, but that seems fast! She could mass-produce her knitwear.

Knowing that I was looking for work, Jackie called me one day and asked if I would be interested in helping her sell knitwear. I would sell knitted hats with company's logos on them. I thought this was a great idea, and I felt confident that I could do it. Because I was not familiar with the sales end of the business, we made plans to meet and discuss it.

After our meeting, I was impressed with her vision and enthusiasm. I agreed wholeheartedly to become a sales representative with her business. My job would be to work from home, calling businesses and taking in knitwear orders. But realistically, I was aware that I was not very good at convincing people to buy things. One time I was having a home interior party and told the ladies that I had invited that they did not have to buy anything. Just come, look, and enjoy my appetizers. Well, of course, those who knew my gift of cooking came, looked, enjoyed my appetizers, and left without ordering anything! Then later my mom admitted even she came just for the food. She only bought the little ivy because she felt guilty. Lesson learned!

The time came to start my job, and I was full of enthusiasm. I turned the dining room table into my makeshift office space. I organized my information sheets, business phone lists and telephone neatly in its place. Before you start scratching your head, wondering why I was doing things that way, it was only 1984, and there were no computers. Then I set my "cheat sheet" in front of me. Finally, I placed the knitted hat samples around the table to have a businesslike feel. With much anticipation, I was ready to make my first business call. I settled into my chair and took a deep breath. *Am I nervous?* I wondered. I picked up the receiver and dialed the first company on my list.

"Hello, Peterson's Dental Office," someone said on the other end of the line.

I had dialed the wrong number! "Oh, for goodness's sake," I said as I hung up.

As I dialed the correct number, I realized that I was sweating. I quickly hung up, thinking I should have a glass of water near me. *Now with water at my side*, I was ready! Once again, I dialed the number and waited. Finally, someone answered, giving their name, the name of the company, and asked, "May I help you?" A severe case of nerves gripped me, and I choked. "Hello? May I help you?" she said again.

At that point, I am not sure what happened to me, but the anxiety got even worse. I cleared my throat and gave my name. Suddenly, I thought I heard myself asking the lady on the other end if she was busy! She quickly said, "Could you hold, please?"

Instantly, I could hear music playing. I tried to pull myself together, searching my cheat sheet for key words, which had now become mumble-jumble. The music disappeared, and she was back on the line. Words were coming from my mouth: "hat," "logo," "umm," "umm."

Apparently, I was not making any sense because she interrupted me, saying, "Ma'am, just what do you want?"

Absolutely mortified, I began to apologize for disturbing her and hung up to save myself any more embarrassment. My forehead was covered with beads of sweat, and my underarms were dripping rivulets down my sides. I sat stunned. *What just happened?* I wondered, knowing full well what it was. Consequently, the makeshift office disappeared from the table and was replaced by a bowl of fake fruit. To this day, I burst out laughing when I think back at my attempt to be a sales rep.

My failure did not stop Jackie. She went on to successfully sell her knitwear. She sold from craft fairs to clothing stores, even setting up a booth at the Minnesota State Fair. In one season, she sold over three thousand hats for a string of daycare facilities. She now knits hats, scarves, and Christmas stockings as a ministry.

It was clear; sales was not one of my strong points. I came to the safe conclusion that cooking was *my* "niche." And so it was!

CHAPTER EIGHTEEN

FLYING CHICKEN BONES

ONE DAY A COUPLE FROM our church called and asked if I would cater their wedding reception. I was thrilled because this would be my first real catering job—other than for family and friends. I immediately said yes. Then the couple announced the wedding is in four weeks! My excitement wilted because I had never catered an event that large before, and I knew I would need a lot of time! As they explained their reasons for the sudden wedding plans, I thought about the amount of experience I would gain from the job. Now with more information, I agreed to do the event.

The following day I met with them to go over the details of the reception and plan the menu. The bride excitedly asked for her favorite dish—chicken curry on rice. Wanting to please her yet never having made it before, I hesitantly agreed to it.

After we were done with our meeting and they had left, I asked myself what chicken curry even was. I had never even heard of it! When I got home, I called my mom and then my mother-in-law to see if they had ever made it. I found out they had never used curry in all their years of cooking. I turned to my many cookbooks, discovering no such recipe! With a flash of inspiration—I am so clever!—I called the bride and matter-of-factly asked if she would prefer me to use their family recipe. She said they did not have one. My "cleverness" was instantly crushed.

Just when I thought I was doomed on my first catering job, tucked between my cookbooks was another tiny cookbook—not much more than a pamphlet—called *Dishes from Around the World*. On page ten: Indian chicken curry on rice! I let out a yell, like I had just won the lottery! I tore the page out of the book and stuck it to the refrigerator with a magnet. The groceries were bought, details were finalized, and plans were made with my friend Coleen to help at the reception. The next day was my first real catering job, and I was ready—or so I thought.

I woke up on the morning of the "big day," feeling sure and confident. All I had to do was prepare the food at home and then take it to the church. The dinner was at two o'clock. I had finished my cup of morning coffee and made breakfast for the kids when I noticed the time. Where had the morning gone? Time was racing by, and I needed to get started. Opening the refrigerator, I saw *twelve* whole fresh chickens staring at me. I needed to get cooking!

Rummaging through my cupboards I could only find *two* cooking pots. It only took moments to figure out I could only fit four chickens in the pots! Now out came the frying pans. With six chickens now cooking, I could relax, even though six more sat in the fridge.

Chicken bubbled and boiled, steaming up the kitchen. "Why are you taking so long to cook?" I snapped at the chickens as if they were testing my patience.

At last, the first batch was done, then the second; but they still needed to be deboned! I glanced at the clock, and my nerves started to unravel. I soon discovered that deboning *hot* chicken took some time! My now burning fingers could not work fast enough. I took a break and started the rice. I still needed to prepare the curry sauce, change clothes, load the car, and drive ten minutes to the church, and then I still had to set up! The reception dinner was only two hours away! I hurried to the refrigerator to get my recipe, and it was gone. I frantically looked under, over, and above the refrigerator, searching everywhere in my kitchen—it was nowhere to be found! Panic seized me in its merciless grip, and my breathing was coming fast and labored. My eyes raced around the kitchen, taking in all that needed to be done. I needed help—NOW!

I called Coleen. "Chicken … recipe … help!" was all she heard.

Minutes later, she stood in my kitchen ready to dive in. I only had an hour and thirty minutes until dinner was to be served! I quickly tossed gloves at Coleen. In moments, all you could see was "flying chicken bones." Finally finished deboning, Coleen grabbed the rice and drove to church. With my head still spinning and time ticking away, I stood in my kitchen covered in chicken with no recipe in sight.

With no time to spare, I began to toss the ingredients that I had bought into the pot of broth leftover from cooking the chicken. Adding a scoop of this and a pinch of that, I guessed my way through it. Last, I held the jar of curry in my hand, wishing someone could just tell me how much to put in. A bad guess could ruin the whole dinner. I nervously added what I thought was the right amount and then grabbed the pot of curried chicken and ran out the door to the car. Shifting my car into drive, I looked down at myself and realized I had not even changed my clothes. I was an absolute mess! With no time to spare, I sped down the road. Suddenly, the strong aroma of curry hit me like a fist, causing me to doubt my catering career.

After arriving at the church, I set the pot on the stove to cook while I prepared the buffet. Soon the ceremony was over, and the bride and groom, along with their guests, were on their way up to the buffet table. Running down the hall with the pot of chicken curry, I prayed I would not trip. Just as I poured it into the chafer, which was on the buffet. It dawned on me that I had not even tasted it yet!

As the last of the one hundred guests made it through the buffet line, I retreated to the kitchen. I found a chair and collapsed! I looked over at Coleen and asked with a sense of dread, "How am I going to explain my chicken curry?" Feeling desperate and hopeless, I wanted to hide.

Before long, the first of the guests were leaving and walking past the kitchen. To my surprise, a couple stuck their heads in and said, "Great job, girls!"

Then another couple said, "Wonderful food, ladies!"

Soon more guests and family members were stopping and showering us with compliments and thanking us for a great meal.

Then unprepared for what was next, a guest leaned into the kitchen and asked, "Who made the chicken curry?"

With hesitation, I told her that I did. A slight smile played across her face and then with a tone of hesitancy, asked, "Would you share your recipe with me?"

Not knowing what to say and not even remembering the ingredient amounts, I replied, "I'm sorry, but it's a secret family recipe."

Five years had passed since that first catering job, and it was while our family was moving when I came across that long-lost recipe for chicken curry. It had fallen under the refrigerator and had been sucked up against the motor. I held it in my hands for a moment, contemplating whether to save it. I quickly tossed it away as I already had *the best chicken curry recipe ever.*

CHAPTER NINETEEN

MY FRIEND BERTHA

I HAVE BEEN BLESSED WITH many friendships in my life, but there was one that was especially dear to my heart. Her name was Bertha Anderson. With a name like Bertha, you could guess she was up in age; but was a petite woman—not at all the stereotype image her name created. She had sparse silver hair set in soft curls. Wrinkles formed deep furrows on her face, but somehow they softened with her tender smile.

Bert, as everyone called her, was eighty-five years old when I first was hired to clean house for her and her husband Waldo. At this same time, my son, Steven, was two years old. Bert said it would be fine for me to bring him along when I cleaned. Cleaning for them was a delight, and I never worried that Steven was interfering with my job because they enjoyed the "spark" he brought to their day. They were always happy to see him.

The Andersons lived in a small quaint home in the town of Buffalo, Minnesota. Built in 1937, it was nestled back from the street, lined with old tall elm trees. Waldo had been the town's doctor for forty-two years, and Bert had been a nurse. They were pillars in the community during the early history of the town. They had retired many years before I had the privilege of meeting them.

A few years had passed by, and Waldo and Steven had connected deeply. One sunny afternoon, while I was cleaning, I looked out the window and saw them on the patio, swinging on a bench swing. They were having cookies and enjoying the warm summer day. Suddenly, the chain holding up the swing broke, and it came crashing down with them in it! To my relief, they looked at each other and started laughing.

Just before we left for home that day, I noticed Waldo's hand was hurt. The Band-Aid he was wearing appeared blood-soaked. Before I could react, Waldo caught my eyes and gave a quick shake of his head "no." Then he whispered to me, "I want Steven to only remember the laugh we shared." Up in age, Waldo passed away a few months later.

I continued to clean for Bert. Steven had started first grade, so now it was just Bert and me on cleaning days. Her appreciation of my help grew, even as our friendship grew. The time shared with her far outweighed the pay for cleaning. She would often call me from wherever I was working to the kitchen. "Let's take a break!" she would say, which meant lunchtime.

Cleaning her house ushered me back in time, to another era. With each room unchanged for years, it was tidy, cozy, and filled with love that only decades of family, a good marriage, and God could accomplish. The small kitchen that she had cooked in for sixty years was nostalgic in appearance and peaceful in presence. A wooden table, with place mats and folded napkins, sat in front of the bay window. Right outside the window was a bird feeder covered with pine siskins.

Sitting down for lunch, a prayer was said, and then Bert always recited Psalm 118:24, "This is the day the Lord hath made, let us rejoice and be glad in it."

Bert used plates, bowls, and teacups that had been collected throughout the years. Lunch was usually a simple sandwich or bowl of soup, served with crackers, sauce, and relishes. She served jelly and sauce in delicate little dishes from her china cabinet. I savored every bite.

Butter was something I rarely ate, but at Bert's, it was different. Dipping a butter knife into the emerald green glass butter dish filled with room temperature butter brought a sense of comfort like a cozy blanket. We enjoyed our lunch, watching the birds outside, and we enjoyed each other. Conversation almost always went to our children and our faith. We laughed, joked, reminisced, and made new memories with our time together. During those precious moments, time seemed to slow down for me.

At age eighty-eight, with health issues, Bert was forced to sell her home. I continued to visit her regularly at the care center. Often I would bring Steven with me, which always brightened her day. They would giggle and share a soda. He was now learning to read, so Bert would sit patiently and listen as he slowly read to her. I usually sat to the side, waiting for my turn to visit.

As her health issues increased, near the end of her life, she was put in a hospital. One evening I decided to pay her another visit to hold her hand and tell her how much she meant to me. I wanted to hug her one more time. Opening the door to her room, I peeked in, and my heart sank. The bed was neatly made up, and Bert was gone. A nurse walked up behind me, put her hand on my arm, and said, "Mrs. Anderson has passed away."

I held my breath and quickly walked out of the hospital. I sobbed as I sat in my car. Finally, emotions drained, I headed home. Heading West, I could not help but notice the beautiful sunset before me. Orange, red, and purple were painted across the sky, awakening my memory, reminding me of Bert's favorite scripture: "This is the day the Lord hath made, let us rejoice and be glad in it."

CHAPTER TWENTY

FORGOTTEN

THROUGHOUT THE YEARS, I HAVE discovered techniques for "remembering" something I had to do. One time I pinned a note to my shirt to remind myself I had to clean out the cat litter box. Going to the post office for stamps, the man behind the counter asked me, "Did you clean out the litter box yet?"

Another time I left myself a note to remind me to read "another" note, only to forget to read *any* note! I recall one evening after a busy day, I stopped at the store to pick up groceries. I carried in a note to remind myself not to forget flour. After filling my cart, including the flour, I put the groceries on the conveyor belt to be rung up. I wrote out a check, and the cashier handed me my receipt. I fidgeted with putting the receipt into my wallet as I headed to my car, pushing the cart. I found the car, but when I went to load my groceries, the cart was empty. Rushing back into the store, I found that not only had I forgotten my groceries, they were still sitting on the conveyor belt waiting to be bagged!

One day, after picking up twenty-six dozen dinner rolls from the bakery, I realized I had forgotten my catering shoes and had to turn around and go back home. I ran into the house, got my shoes, and headed for my catering job fifteen miles away. Heading down the highway, I was enjoying the aroma of fresh baked rolls. Suddenly, out from under the seat popped our cat, Vinnie! I knew instantly I had to turn around and take him home. I thought I must have left the car door open when I ran in to get my shoes. Back at the house, I scolded Vinnie for being a bad cat. Because I was now running late, I had to hurry to my catering job. I arrived and quickly opened the back door of the van. With horror, I looked down at the twenty-six dozen dinner rolls. Every single package had deep paw dents! Vinnie had walked all over them! Thankfully, none of the packages were punctured. With no time to get more, I had to serve the squished dinner rolls. I asked my helpers to not "let the cat out of the bag" about the rolls, until one day when I put the story in a book—so here it is!

When my son, Mike, was a teenager he worked for a meat market in our town; I ordered meat from them for my catering business. For one particular job, I ordered 160 pounds of fresh pork roast. I was going to pick it up on Saturday for Sunday's catering event.

That Saturday was extremely busy as I prepared for the big job. By evening, my brain could not think any longer. Though it seemed like I was ready for tomorrow, I went to bed feeling like I had forgotten something. Troubled, I could not think of what it might be. My head hit the soft pillow, and I had no more than closed my eyes when there was a knock on the bedroom door. It was Mike, coming in to say good night. Suddenly, I looked at him in horror as if he had the words "pork roast" written across his forehead! It hit me that I had forgotten to pick up the 160 pounds of pork roast from the meat market! I jumped up from the bed filled with panic. I had to start cooking them early in the morning at my kitchen, and the meat market was closed on Sunday!

Even though it was eleven thirty at night, Mike assured me he could get us into the market. He had been given the keys to lock up that evening. My initial response was "No!" But with the owners probably asleep by now, my desperation took over. I said, "Let's go!" I put on a coat over my pajamas, and we headed to the meat market.

With my heart pounding, I held the flashlight while Mike unlocked the front door. Once inside, Mike turned on the dim hall light, and we walked back to the cooler. Cautiously stepping inside, the cold air took my breath away. Whole skinned hogs and beef hung from hooks that swung eerily as we searched for my order. Once again, like so many times in my life, I felt like I was on a movie set, and this was a scary movie! Then to my relief, we found the cases with my name on them. Then fearing that the police would show up, we quickly loaded the cases onto a cart and wheeled it out to my van. I left a check on the counter with a note that said, "ORDER RECEIVED."

Although the experience seemed like a nightmare, I had to chuckle as I lay back down in bed, trying to imagine what a police officer's response might have been. After all, finding a woman wearing a coat over her pajamas, scrounging inside a meat market with a teenage boy, at midnight, would have been a strange encounter for anyone!

CHAPTER TWENTY-ONE

UNEXPECTED OBSTACLES

I'VE ALWAYS SAID, "DON'T ASK me to figure out documents," that reminds me of taxes; "Don't hand me a lengthy sheet of instructions," that reminds me of the time my son and I tried to put together a gas grill; and "Don't ask me to read through statements," that reminds me of the time I thought the bank owed me $340, when, in fact, I owed them! Give me a thousand people to feed with a day's notice, I can do that! However, along with feeding those one thousand people would also come the *unexpected* obstacles that I have learned to *expect* during my catering career.

One day I was the first to arrive at a hall where I was catering a three hundred-guest wedding reception. I had lots to do before my staff arrived, so I turned on all the ovens to five hundred degrees to heat them up quickly. Then I went out to my van to unload. With the last of my things in my arms, I walked toward the door when a sudden gust of wind blew it shut. Pulling on the handle, I realized, to my horror, that it was a self-locking door! I was locked out, and my purse, keys, and phone were inside! I frantically ran the whole outside of the building, hoping that one door would be found unlocked. No luck. I stood trying to process the fact that I had no phone to call anyone and no keys to go anywhere. Then it dawned on me—it was Memorial weekend— no one was around!

Pressing my nose up against the little window in the door, I could see the clock inside—its hands seemed to be waving at me. With the ovens turned on full blast and time ticking by quickly, I did the only thing I knew to do—PRAY! "Lord, help me!" I pleaded.

As if expecting the door to be opened, I reached for the handle and pulled. Still locked. Then from around the corner of the hall, I saw my sister Kim drive into the parking lot.

As I ran to her car, she got out and said, "I came early, I hope that's okay."

With no time to go into detail or even give her a hug, I asked for her phone. I called city hall. No answer. "Of course!" I snapped. "Everyone is enjoying the holiday!"

At this point, Kim and I decided we had no choice—we had to call 911.

Through my panic-stricken voice, I tried to explain to the 911 operator what had happened. She instantly confirmed with me that all the commercial ovens were turned on at the hall. "Yes! To five hundred degrees!" I added.

She quickly made the decision that this was an emergency and said she would send an officer over. Within minutes, the officer came, with emergency lights on.

Embarrassed, I thanked the officer as he unlocked the door. He made sure that everything inside was okay. I then offered him the only thing I could offer—a buttered dinner roll. He took it and left.

This was an unexpected obstacle in my day, but my prayer was answered. Kim told me later that she had plans to go shopping before coming to the hall, but at the last minute, she changed her mind, thinking, "I better see if Barb needs my help instead." Boy did I ever!

Occasionally, while my son, Steven, played at a baseball tournament, I would have to be at or preparing for a catering job. I hated to miss watching him play. And it was at one game his team was up against another outstanding team. The winner would place in a tournament. It was a critical game, and Steven was the starting pitcher! With no question, I needed to be at that game! Predictably, I had to, once again, prepare for a catering job that was the next day. With thirty-five pounds of fresh green beans that needed to be snapped, I wrestled with how I was going to do this. Soon the van was packed with baseball gear, equipment, and a large cooler filled with green beans!

At the game that evening, I watched my son pitch, and every so often, I would glance over at the team moms—with gloves on, snapping beans, and cheering loudly. That summer evening not only did the green beans get snapped, but our boys also won and went on to place in the tournament!

There was another time I had a catering job, and at the same time, a longtime girlfriend from Texas came home for a short visit. A get-together was planned at the home of our friend, Alise. There are nine of us high school friends who continue to get together thirty-nine years after graduation. Four of the ladies live out of state. To this day, I do not understand why they do because in tenth grade, we made a pact that we would live by one another— forever! We have had some good laughs—like the time Alise, who lives in Minnesota, showed up on Joni's doorstep in Maine and asked if she could borrow a cup of sugar. Another time, Cindy visited our friend, Kim, who lives in New York. They drove to where Woodstock was held and toasted a glass of wine, reminiscing about their lives back in 1969.

We have laughed with one another and shared in one another's tears and hardships. We now celebrate our children's weddings and attend one another's parent's funerals. So you see, when there is an opportunity to get together, we try to let no obstacles get in the way. This was the case for me. I was preparing for a catering job at the same time as one of our get-togethers before Coleen left to go back to Texas. With five hundred croissants that needed slicing, I had to consider my options.

That evening at Alise's house, I asked the girls to gather around the big kitchen table. Unaware of what I was about to do, the girls questioned my craziness as they came to the table. I proceeded to cover the table with a plastic cloth, handed everyone plastic gloves, and set a handful of knives in the center of the table. At this point, they did not know if they should laugh or be afraid! I quickly went out to my van and came back carrying the first of many containers of croissants.

That night we laughed, shared our problems, humored one another in our walk-through menopause and sliced croissants. Suddenly, Julie set her knife down and said, "If you had told me forty years ago that we would be sitting around slicing croissants and talking menopause, I'd have thought you were crazy!"

I replied, "Julie, we would not have known what menopause was!"

In a moment of silence, everyone stopped to consider that; and then with smiles and shrugs of agreement, we continued to slice away.

CHAPTER TWENTY-TWO

THE LAUGH THAT WAS HEARD FOR MILES

MY FRIEND COLEEN AND I have shared wonderful times together, especially when we were pregnant at the same time. We have also been at each other's sides during difficult times. But one seemingly normal day, at one bizarre moment, we laughed so hard, tears streamed down our faces.

It all started one day while driving from Minnesota to Williston, North Dakota. If you have ever driven that stretch of highway, you know how boring that drive can be. After five hours of conversation, we were talked out. So we became quiet, absorbed in our thoughts with still a few more hours to drive.

While Coleen drove, I sat listening to the soothing rumble of the motor. Suddenly, a thought came to mind. I remembered a true story I had heard from my sister about one of her clients. It was an embarrassing moment with someone passing gas. I decided to tell it to Coleen, which led to an hour of laughing over many shared "passed-gas" stories.

As we were coming into a town, Coleen saw that we needed to fuel up. She pulled into a gas station, and while she finished pumping gas, I ran into the station to use the restroom. While in the bathroom, Coleen came in and went into the stall down from me. Remembering the stories, we had just shared in the car, I laughed and said, "Now I do not want to hear any farting over there. No farting allowed!"

There was silence. Then as I slowly stepped out of the stall, the door near mine opened. There stood a woman with eyes piercing me like daggers. Horribly embarrassed, I splashed water on my hands and ran out, my face beet red. There, by the car, washing the windows was Coleen. Not having a clue what just happened, she looked at me and froze. Running for the car and looking like I had just robbed the store, I yelled, "Let's go!"

She sped out of the station lot as I started to tell her about the "no farting instructions" I had just given a stranger!

The last hours of our trip went by fast as every once in a while, Coleen would burst out laughing as she tried to imagine the look on that woman's face—sitting on the toilet and a stranger telling her not to fart.

That summer, while Coleen and I were attending a women's retreat, I shared that story with a large group of ladies. It brought a lot of laughs. One woman in particular thought that was the funniest story ever. When she got home, she told her husband.

Twenty years had passed since that embarrassing day at the gas station. I had finally forgotten about it. But one day it came to light again in a surprising and unusual way.

I was catering a wedding reception for an unknown couple that lived sixty miles away. While preparing the buffet, I was surprised to see someone I had not seen for twenty years, and we greeted each other. As we talked, he reminded me about "the farting story." He was the husband of the woman at the retreat that had thought it was the funniest story ever. As we stood in the kitchen laughing, his eyes suddenly lit up, and he became ecstatic.

"Wait here! Don't move!" he ordered.

Before long, he came back into the kitchen, pulling another gentleman by the shirt. He planted the confused looking man right in front of me and said with excitement, "This … is … the lady … that started the farting story!"

The man, standing in front of me, took my hands in his, looked me in the eyes, and with amazement, said, "I am a motivational speaker and travel the United States and all over the world. I use the farting story as an ice breaker at all my seminars!"

It was my turn to be amazed. Who would have ever thought that this silly little story would be told all over the world?

CHAPTER TWENTY-THREE

LOAVES AND FISHES— FOR FOUR HUNDRED

AS I PREPARED FOR MY usual Monday school lunches, I thought about the plans for Friday's catering job. A very hectic week was staring me in the face. A sense of anxiety was building, so it was not such a great shock when things began to go wrong. Then what unfolded in the end had me appreciating even more one of Jesus's great miracles.

I had just gotten home from feeding two hundred students and staff at school. Tired, I kicked my shoes off, grabbed a cup of coffee, and headed for my favorite chair to relax. As I passed the answering machine, I decided to check my messages. I listened as I took a sip of coffee and looked over at my comfy chair, which seemed to be calling to me. At that moment, I did not realize I would not even be able to finish the coffee, much less sit and relax.

There was a beep that I had another new message. A woman calmly said, "Hi, Barb, this is Kate. I just want to give you a head count for this Friday, for the wedding reception."

Wedding? I thought, puzzled. *I have a Christmas party this Friday!*

The message continued, "We are planning four hundred people for my daughter's reception."

Suddenly, my knees went weak, and I set my cup of coffee down.

Her message ended with, "Call me when you can. Otherwise, I'll see you Friday."

My heart began to pound its way out of my chest. I went to my office and looked at my calendar. Nothing. I flung open my catering work order book. Nothing about a wedding on Friday—just the Christmas party. Perplexed, I wondered why this all sounded so familiar. Turning my wastebasket over, I tore through the trash, looking for any clues. My heart stopped. There on the bottom of the can was a proposal, written over the phone—three months ago! I quickly remembered that I never had gotten a response back or a deposit to secure the date as requested, and so when catering, a Christmas party, came up for December 15, I called Kate to double check I was not needed and left a message. Days later, still not having heard back from her, I threw away the proposal and accepted the Christmas party job. It was clear I did not double-book an event, so I was relieved. But now I had to make a difficult phone call and let Kate know I could not cater the reception—less than a week away!

There was no answer when I made the call, so I left a message again for her to call me immediately. Hours went by, and I was becoming concerned as it was Monday evening, and the wedding was now only four days away. She would have an extremely difficult time finding a caterer on such short notice. Finally, she returned the call. I answered and heard a trembling voice say, "Tell ... me ... you are ... catering ... my ... daughter's ... reception ... this ... Friday."

With all the compassion I had, I answered, "No."

I explained why, and at the same time, she realized her mistake of assuming without communicating. We knew it would be virtually impossible to find a caterer at this point— short notice, four hundred people, and it was Christmas! My heart broke for her. With no promise whatsoever, I told her I would call the only caterer I knew. As expected, they too were booked solid.

I sat at my office desk with my face buried in my hands. I had to call her back. Suddenly, a glimmer of hope flickered in my mind. Perhaps I could arrange my schedule so I could cater the wedding reception *and* the Christmas party! But I had to keep in mind that I was also doing school lunch that day. I sat and feverishly worked on a plan. I realized the whole thought of trying to do this was completely insane!

I called my daughter, Missy, who had helped me cater throughout the years. Even though she had never catered a job on her own, she was willing to set up and serve at the Christmas party as long as I had prepared all the appetizers. I then called the client having the Christmas party and explained what had happened. She agreed to let Missy cater; however, she would expect her to do a good job as I would. Even though I trusted Missy, I felt a huge wave of uneasiness come over me. I began to swivel back and forth in my chair as I contemplated my decision. I prayed and asked for God's direction. Before I knew it, the phone was in my hand, and I was dialing Kate. As I gave her the good news and shared my plan, she cried. She responded with relief and thankfulness. That night, as I lay in bed, my head swam. The reality of having only three days to prepare for a Christmas party, a reception for four hundred, *and* serve school lunch that day for two hundred students had me praying!

Tuesday through Thursday, I served school lunches and made "to-do" lists. Staff was hired, and groceries were bought. Most of the food for the reception was ordered through my food distributor. It was going to be delivered to my kitchen on Friday—the day of the wedding! It was crucial that the order be delivered on time. By Thursday night, I was exhausted.

Friday, I woke up early and knew it was going to be a sink-or-swim day, so I asked for God's life jacket. This was how Friday, December 15, unfolded: In the morning, I prepared the school lunch; my new friend Lori, from the coffee shop, would arrive at school to help serve lunch and then come with me to the reception. Unexpectedly, I received a call from my food distributor, saying the delivery truck missed the stop at my kitchen and would not be able to return for *three hours!* The reception started *in less than six hours!*

Back at my kitchen, my brain was on overload as I continued to make appetizers for the Christmas party. Thinking about all that needed to be done made the job of hand-stuffing mushrooms and skewering chicken satays all the more unnerving. I had to force myself to stop looking at the clock every few minutes, so I could finish with all the appetizers and pack the van for Missy.

"Where's the delivery truck?" I yelled, realizing I had not even started to pack anything for the reception, which was now in three hours!

At last, the delivery truck pulled up. As it did, Ed arrived from work, and behind him came Missy. With no time to spare, we literally threw everything into the van so Missy could be on time for the Christmas party. As she was pulling away from the curb, I was shouting directions on how to get there. The food from the delivery truck was quickly tossed into the back of Ed's truck. Lori, now done with school lunch, and my son, Steven, arrived and got into the truck. I ran around the kitchen, grabbing seasonings, utensils, and aprons before running out the door. Ed's truck was in forward motion as I jumped in. Catching my breath, I realized it would be nearly impossible to make chicken wild rice soup for four hundred hungry people.

On the way to the reception, I gave everyone their jobs as there would be no time for questions. After arriving and while the others unloaded the truck, I ran around the kitchen and reception area to get a firsthand look at what the layout was. Back in the kitchen, I quickly lined up six big stock pots for the soup. With no time to measure anything I just divided up the frozen diced chicken, cooked wild rice, commercial cans of broth and condensed soup, diced onion and celery and threw in random seasonings. Because the heat was turned up to full blast, Ed stood by and stirred. We had to serve in one hour!

Lori and I were cutting up fresh fruit when, suddenly, my phone rang. It was Missy, and she was lost! Panic set in as I tried to remember the directions. Then to my horror, I watched as the bottom of the big box of breadsticks Steven was holding fell open! A fourth of the breadsticks were now on the floor! Forgetting that Missy was on the phone, I ran to help Steven. With no time to clean up the mess, we kicked the bread to the side. Looking down, I realized I still had the phone in my hand and shouted, "Missy!"

She had hung up. Could she find her way? Did I have enough breadsticks? I spun around and looked over at the pots of soup. Did I have enough soup?

I hurried out to the reception area to finish setting up the buffet. When I came through the doors, it seemed there were a thousand people looking at me as if to say, "We are hungry!"

Then while trying to pull myself together, a woman approached me and asked if I was the caterer. With a blank look, I numbly said, "Yes."

"I heard you double-booked these people," she said, glaring at me.

Suddenly, words were caught at the tip of my tongue that I did not want to let fly, and I began to break down. I quickly turned and went back into the kitchen. Instantly, I called everyone to the center of the kitchen and announced, "We need God's help!" We held hands and prayed, "Lord, calm me. Also, be with Missy. And just as you fed four thousand with seven loaves of bread and a few fish, I ask that you stretch this soup to feed all these people." Together, we said, "Amen." I looked up and ordered, "Let's do this!"

Lori ran with the first bowls of fruit, Steven behind her with the baskets of breadsticks, and I followed with bowls of salad. Just as the wedding party was coming up to the buffet, Ed carried in the first of the soup. While in a state of frenzy, we ran back and forth from the kitchen to the buffet, replenishing the fruit, salad, bread and soup, and more soup, and more soup! Soon Ed scraped the last of the soup from the last stock pot and set it on the buffet. To our amazement, we all stood by watching as the last guest took the last breadstick, picked through the last of the fruit and spooned out the last helping of soup.

Back in the kitchen, we celebrated, giving each other high-fives. Suddenly, my phone rang— it was Missy! "Letting you know, Mom, that everything is going well." I leaned against the wall with a sigh of relief.

As my staff finished cleaning the kitchen, I went back to the buffet table. There was one thing I simply had to know: How many of the supposedly four hundred people came through the buffet? With Steven by my side, I counted 335 bowls that were taken. Steven asked, "Where were the other sixty-five people?"

I laughed and said, "Some were probably stuck in traffic, some probably changed their minds and went fishing, and others ..." Then I looked up toward heaven and whispered, "After all, I only had soup for 335!"

CHAPTER TWENTY-FOUR

TADPOLE IN A HOLE

YEARS AGO, WHEN MY DAUGHTER, Missy, was about eight years old, she received a cookbook for her birthday from her grandma. The book was filled with recipes for young children. There was one recipe that caught Missy's attention.

Like me, when I was young, Missy loved nature. She was fascinated with anything that resembled creeping-crawling. One day, while our family was at a park, her brother, Mike, stepped on and squashed a beetle that was crossing the parking lot.

Angry, Missy stomped over to Mike, stuck her hands on her hips, and hollered, "Mike, think before you kill!" She thought all insects had a right to live.

With this in mind, I was not surprised when the first recipe she wanted to make was "TADPOLE IN A HOLE."

Reading through the recipe, I was relieved that I did not have to go to the bait shop as the tadpoles were actually pieces of sausage. With all the ingredients on hand, I helped her prepare the first recipe. Then she anxiously stood by the oven while it baked. Finally, the aroma of the sweet corn bread, sausage, and cheese filled the air. That night, while our family sat enjoying the yummy dish, Missy proudly reminded us that she had made it herself.

Months later, I decided to make her recipe for supper again. While taking out all the ingredients, I realized I had no sausage to make the "tadpoles." Contemplating what to do, I remembered we had venison sausage in the freezer. The deer had been processed after Ed hit and killed it while driving. I could use the venison instead and not tell anybody. That evening we gathered at the table for supper. I set the dish on the table and served it up.

Suddenly, Mike spoke up and said, "This sausage looks different!"

Reluctantly, I confessed to them that it was the sausage from the deer.

Then as boys will be boys, he snickered and said, "Look, Missy, we're not eating tadpoles, we're eating 'roadkill' in a hole!"

Devastated, Missy ran to her room. I quickly put my finger to my lips to shush everyone, but we could not contain ourselves. We silently laughed until we cried.

It has been many years since that time, and now Missy prepares the dish for her two boys. One weekend, while the boys were visiting, I decided to make "tadpole in a hole." With enthusiasm, the boys wanted to help prepare it. As we poured the corn bread batter into the pan and then added the sausage to the top, I shared that story with them. Naturally, they found it very amusing and requested to hear it over—and over again.

This recipe has not only been a comfort food to our family, but it also had delighted us with a treasured story for years. May you enjoy it as well. I thought you might also enjoy the recipe!

TADPOLE IN A HOLE

One 8 oz. box of Jiffy corn bread mix

One 12 oz. can of whole kernel corn—plus liquid

One egg

2½ cups of shredded cheddar cheese

One 1 lb. pkg. Jimmy Dean Sausage (or venison!) thawed

In a medium bowl, add the corn bread mix, can of corn with liquid, the egg, and one cup of cheese. Mix, then pour into a nine-by-thirteen-inch baking dish. Pull apart the uncooked sausage and arrange on top of the batter. Sprinkle remaining cheese on top. Bake at 350° for thirty minutes.

CHAPTER TWENTY-FIVE

CAKE CRAZY

I MUST ADMIT—I LOVE CAKE! I am crazy about it. Not dry, powdered, sugar-dusted cakes, but moist, mounded-high-with-frosting cakes. Over the years, while catering, my staff would laugh at me because I would not eat what I prepared. My focus would be sitting out on a table in the reception area—the cake. However, there would be times when I would go out to check the reception area and find that all the cake was gone! "No!" I would then try to hide my disappointment.

My sweet tooth comes from my deep Scandinavian blood. I come from a long line of sweet-tooth cravers! My dad is in a category all of its own, especially when you add coffee to the mix.

When my children were younger, I made all their birthday cakes; and they were not just any ordinary cakes either. For the fourth birthday of my daughter, Missy, I made a "Care Bear" cake. It sat eighteen inches high. When she saw the cake, the expression on her face was priceless. And when it came time to cut it, she cried!

One time I made a "tent" cake for Jeremy's eighth birthday because he loved to camp. I added a picnic table and a campfire made from unwrapped tootsie rolls; a tea candle was placed in the middle for the campfire. After the fire was lit, and the kids were finishing the birthday song, one of the tootsie rolls started on fire! Thinking it was part of the cake, the kids cheered and clapped!

For the birthday of my son, Mike, I made an orange school bus. As I set the cake in front of him, the Oreo cookie wheels collapsed from the moisture of the cake! Mike was disheartened. I quickly assured him that the tires just needed to be changed, so I put new Oreos on.

By the time our fourth child, Steven, came along, life was busy, so baking creative cakes happened less often. On one of his birthdays, I set a simple cake in front of him, and by the look on his face, I could tell something was wrong. Finally, he let us know that his brothers and sister had cooler cakes than he did. Teasingly, his dad said, "That's because we like them more than you." Aware of his popularity in the family, Steven only smiled.

Adding to my many cake creations, I have made a real-to-life computer cake, a dinosaur cake, and a cake in the shape of a shirt. One time I made a birthday cake for my brother-in-law that looked like a big chunk of Swiss cheese, with little mice coming out of the holes! Written on top was "To the Big Cheese." However, my brother-in-law, who is afraid of mice, would not eat it as it was too creepy!

Also, in my adventure of making cakes, I have had the privilege of making cakes for many personal celebrations. To my delight, I made my daughter's wedding cake and my own twenty-fifth wedding anniversary cake. Then by the time my grandsons came along, my cakes had become more predictable and ordinary. My grandson, Austin, and I still laugh about the cake I made him years ago. One day I told him that I would make a cake for his seventh birthday. He put in his order of chocolate cake, chocolate frosting, and race cars on top; but as the days got busier for me, time to make it was running out. Staying up late the night before the party, I got started. Everything went wrong! First, the cake fell in the middle, then the frosting was pulling up the top of the cake, and the frosting application bag kept clogging, which made the words "Happy Birthday" unreadable. At last, while setting the cars on top, I noticed one of the cars was broken, so I arranged them to sort of look like they had crashed. Despite my best efforts, the cake was a failure.

The next day at the party, Austin sat eagerly waiting for me to bring the cake in from the car. As I carried it up the driveway, I hesitated and thought, *Maybe I should tell him I forgot it, or maybe I dropped it and then run to the grocery store and buy one.*

All this ran through my mind as I came through the door. Coming up the stairs, I could see him jumping with excitement. I lifted the cover, and suddenly, his excitement turned to a look of disbelief. The room became silent. Then he looked up at me and said matter-of-factly, "That's okay, Grandma, you can make me a better one next year."

Bursts of laughter filled the room as the candles were being lit.

Along with fond memories, I have also experienced terrifying and anxious moments that only a nightmare could hold. One time Kathy and I were preparing a wedding reception dinner down in a church basement, while the ceremony took place upstairs. A man came to deliver and set up the wedding cake. When he was done, he handed the bill to me and left.

We decided to walk over to the cake to take a peek. Walking toward it, we quickly saw that it was slowly leaning to the side and ready to fall over! Stepping up our pace, we set it upright and secured it. However, on further inspection, we could see that the cake dividers and pillars that separated the three tiers were yellowed and worn with age. Concerned that the delivery man did not remember to finish decorating in between or around the tiers, we decided to fix the problem ourselves. We reluctantly took one daisy from each vase sitting on the guest tables and arranged them in between the tiers and then added greens around the base. It looked lovely.

Shortly, the family and guests came down, and we held our breath; not knowing if we did the right thing. Almost at once, there were "oohs" and "aahs" as they gathered around the cake. One of the grandmas said in astonishment, "That is the prettiest cake I have ever seen!"

Later we made the mother of the bride aware of what had happened.

On another wedding occasion, while I was catering, someone had come up to me and asked about serving the cake. Although cake-cutting is not our responsibility, if needed, we can help. Just to be sure, I asked this person to go ask the bride and groom if they were ready to do so. Now I am not exactly sure how the sequence of miscommunication went—all I know is I was given permission to cut the cake. And cut it—I did—every layer! As I dutifully sliced and plated the cake, guests were swiftly taking it. Suddenly, while looking down, I heard a loud gasp. I turned and looked up, and there stood the bride and groom. By the look on their faces, I knew what the gasp was about. Not only did they not get a picture of feeding each other the first slice, but also there had not been any pictures of the cake at all! Later I questioned myself, did my love for cake push me into a cake-cutting frenzy, or was it a miscommunication? I am sure I heard "cut the cake."

One time, during another cake disaster, I walked into a hall to cater, only to see two layers—including the top of the wedding cake—on the floor! I soon had to plead my innocence as it was insinuated that it may have been my fault. But later they apologized because they found no support pegs in the cake to hold it up.

I thought, *Why would I be negligent? Less cake means "no cake" for me!*

Of all the cake memories, there is one that stands out the most, the one that nearly had me crawling into a hole to hide.

I had worked for Susan in her home, babysitting and helping with her dinner parties for three years. Her beautiful Persian features were as stunning as her beautiful, elegant home. Her husband was a highly respected surgeon. It was the evening of their daughter's first birthday party. Susan is an amazing cook and prepared a lovely dinner for all the guests. Dressed in crisp black and white uniforms, I and my friend Coleen were hired to help serve it, along with the appetizers and cocktails.

Before the guests arrived, Susan gave us instructions and explained how she wanted the birthday cake presented. I was to bring the cake in from the back patio and set it on the dining room table, while everyone was in the living room for the gift opening. So after the dining room table was cleared from dinner, Coleen opened the bottles of wine while I went to get the cake. I stood in amazement as I stared down at the most beautiful cake I had ever seen. As I slowly slid my hands underneath the mammoth cake, I could feel the weight of it. While lifting it, I intuitively knew there should be two people moving it. With the weight of it on my arms, I wondered how I was going to open the door. Not wanting to yell, I cautiously managed, all the while telling myself, "Don't drop it, don't trip."

Moving very carefully, I made my way through the family room, down a long wide hall, and into the dining room. I moved slowly as I approached the table, gently setting it down and cautiously pulling my arms out from underneath it.

"Whew!" I breathed a sigh of relief. Then I noticed that the cake was sitting too close to the edge of the table. I then contemplated, *Should I move it over?*

And of course, I just had to move it and make it perfect. Pushing the cake tray, my hand slipped forward, causing my hand to rip through the entire six-layer cake—exposing the ganache and cream fillings, flattening the delicate sugar-dipped fruits and flowers and messing up the last letters of "Happy Birthday!"

Suddenly, Susan peeked around the door and said, "We're just about ready to come in— light the candle."

Was there a candle? I hardly noticed. Almost in tears, I ran into the kitchen, gesturing to Coleen to come. She gasped at the sight. We frantically repaired the cake as best we could. Sweat was running down my brow as I lit the candle. I could hear Susan and her guest coming down the hall. Coleen and I went back into the kitchen, and I waited to hear a scream. Suddenly, after the birthday song was done, Susan came into the kitchen. Before I could say one word, she said, in her beautiful Persian accent, "Barbara, what happened to the cake?"

Trying to explain, through my shaking voice, she reached over and gave me a hug. "Please serve the wine—and don't spill it," she said with a smile. I made sure I didn't.

With all the anxious moments and frightful experiences involving cake, you would think that I would dislike cake, but to this day, I am still cake-crazy! My only question is, "Do you think there'll be cake in heaven?" Because I really do like angel food cake!

CHAPTER TWENTY-SIX

KATHLEEN

MANY FASCINATING STORIES DEVELOPED AND cherished memories resulted from my catering career. However, one story convinced me that God puts people into our lives to impact us in profound ways. This story is about a person I hardly knew—her name was Kathleen.

One afternoon, while sitting at my desk, I received a phone call. The woman on the other end told me her name was Kathleen. She shared that she had been praying for the right caterer. Then one day a friend had given her my name and phone number, but only after seeking God's direction did she call me. We discussed the date, time, and location of the event. I checked my calendar to find that the day had not been booked yet. She hired me immediately, which was a surprise because most new clients wanted background information about my services and references. After all that, they would get back to me to secure the date.

Just as we started to talk about the menu, I realized that she had not mentioned what the occasion was. I politely interrupted her and inquired. With a soft, despondent tone of voice, she replied, "You will be catering my celebration of life dinner."

Not sure what that was, I asked, "What do you mean?"

She slowly responded, "I am dying."

Nothing could have prepared me for that answer. I swallowed hard and told her I would be honored to do the dinner. For the next hour, we discussed the details and planned the menu for her celebration. Because of the circumstances, it was difficult to bring up the cost—it suddenly seemed trivial to me, even though I needed the income. The subject came up, and we agreed on an amount; a deposit was made. We shared a little about ourselves and finally said goodbye. I hung up the phone and leaned back in my chair. I wondered what it would feel like to plan the end of your life. As I stared out the window and pondered her situation, I was amazed at her courage.

Weeks passed since our phone conversation. I decided to get some exercise and have some quiet time to think. As I was walking on my favorite path, Kathleen came to mind, and my heart was moved to pray for her and her family. My heartfelt compassion compelled me to make sure everything was going to be perfect for her celebration dinner.

Days later, I was walking the path again. Moving through the open field, the sun felt warm on my face. I once again thought of Kathleen. I began talking to the Lord about her upcoming dinner. "Prepare me, Lord, for the upcoming task. Help me to bless her."

Suddenly, my attention was stirred, and I suddenly stopped on the path I was walking, and it became clear—I was to cater Kathleen's dinner without charge. I assumed that God was blessing Kathleen and her husband.

I continued down the path, aware that I was verbally protesting. I said, "But, Lord, the income from this job is needed!"

After expressing my reason for concern, my mind was quieted. After all, I realized that what God wanted for Kathleen was far more important. He would take care of our needs.

On the evening of the celebration dinner, Ed, my son Steven, who was now fifteen, and I arrived at the hall. We were quickly greeted by Kathleen's husband, Rick. He introduced us to the family. Anxious to meet Kathleen, Rick brought her over to us. She was a very petite woman in her forties and had an amazing, beautiful smile. We hugged as if we had known each other for years. With lots to do to make the dinner happen, we went to the kitchen to start the preparations. Soon the guests began to arrive, and the hall filled with 150 of Kathleen's family and friends. We served a beautiful buffet with many of her favorite foods. Throughout the evening, people of all ages stood and shared the memories they had of Kathleen. As we cleared the buffet and cleaned up, we were blessed by the many stories we heard.

I knew that Kathleen's husband would soon be coming into the kitchen to pay me for the dinner. I asked the Lord to prepare me, and at that moment, Rick walked in with his checkbook in hand. Ed and Steven waited by the door, ready to leave. Because they did not know my "payment plan," I asked them to wait outside in the van.

He began by thanking me for the wonderful dinner. "It couldn't have been more perfect!" he said with a smile and proceeded to take his pen out.

I quickly motioned for him to sit down on the nearby stool. "I have something I want to share with you."

I began to describe to him my experience walking on the path and what God had spoken to me. I looked into his eyes, took the checkbook, and closed it in his hands. "This dinner is God's gift to Kathleen. He just used me to serve it."

A wave of emotion overcame him as the impact of what I had said dawned on him. Tears welled up in his eyes. "Can I at least pay for part of the catering?" he asked.

Wanting Rick to understand God's love and plan, I said, "If I took anything, I would take away what God wants for Kathleen. I would be disobedient to my Lord."

I hugged him and told him to go back in and enjoy his time with family, friends, and most of all, Kathleen. We hugged again and said goodbye.

I left the hall, closing the door behind me, and jumped into the van. Ed pulled away from the curb and headed down the street. Concerned by my expression, he asked if everything was all right. Steven leaned forward from the back seat and asked how much money he had made tonight. I took a breath and said, "Tonight we served for God."

I then proceeded to share the whole story with them. Silence filled the van for the next few miles.

Steven leaned forward again and thoughtfully said, "That's cool, Mom."

Ed added, "That's awesome!"

We rode the rest of the way home in silence as the impact of the night overwhelmed us.

Time had passed since that night, and the busyness of everyday life overshadowed our memory of the evening, throwing unexpected challenges and circumstances at us. One afternoon I sat at my desk, fretting over the pile of unexpected bills sitting in front of me. They needed to be paid, but the money was not there. I stopped and simply talked to my Lord, thanking Him for His love and provision. Worry seemed to melt away in the light of His presence. I paid what I could and had peace about the situation. I had just licked the last stamp and put it on the envelope when the phone rang. It was Rick—Kathleen had passed away. He asked if I could cater the lunch at the funeral. Naturally, I agreed, and plans were made.

The next morning the doorbell rang, and I answered it. A courier handed me an envelope with my name on it. Wondering what it was, I quickly opened it. I was stunned when I saw a check, written out to me from Rick. My knees went weak. The substantial amount written out took my breath away! Steven walked over to me to see what had me standing there stunned. With tears streaming down my face, I looked at him and said, "I want you to remember this moment, because God has just revealed His extraordinary and amazing grace to me!" He took the check from my hand, and then we stood there stunned.

Later that day, after buying all the food needed for the funeral, I decided to pay all our bills— IN FULL! However, it was not until I totaled the groceries and all the bills that I was hit by the startling realization that it was the exact amount written on the check!

That evening I called Rick and struggled to find the words to thank him. He suddenly stopped me and said, "Barb, Kathleen and I prayed about it, and the Lord made it clear what the amount of the check was to be." Then he added, "That's His blessing to you!"

CHAPTER TWENTY-SEVEN

TWENTY-EIGHT MINUTES

EVERY YEAR I RECEIVE A phone call from Jodi who works for a law firm. She requests my catering services for the company's summer family picnics. I had always thought that if I ever had to change careers, I would want to work for this one law firm, even if I were to just maintain the coffee area. This company loves to have fun! I have had the opportunity to cater for them several times, and each picnic usually starts out with a competitive game of softball.

One August day Jodi called and hired me to cater their company family hayride and picnic they were having in October. We created a hardy menu of pulled-pork sandwiches, baked beans, coleslaw, chips, and cookies. We decided to serve hot coffee and hot apple cider just in case the weather had taken a chilly turn.

The night before the big event, the weather forecasters were saying that winds had shifted and that we may get cooler temperatures the following day. The next morning they said that winds would pick up later in the day. Jodi and I talked that morning and decided that we were all true Minnesotans, and we could handle a little diversity in the weather. Besides, they were not going to let a little weather hinder their day of fun! As usual, I prepared the food but hoped the weather would cooperate as there was no shelter in the area.

Steven and I were loading up the van with catering supplies and food when I looked up and grimaced at what looked like sleet coming down! The wind picked up and had us shivering. We didn't really expect to see anyone when we arrived at our destination, but to our surprise, we could just make out a tractor chugging toward us, pulling a hay wagon. As it pulled into the farmyard, I glanced at my watch. They had come back early. We watched from the van, wondering how many people were under the mountain of blankets—now covered with sleet. Only a few brave dads kept their heads exposed.

Suddenly, the wind began to howl as Jodi jumped off the wagon and ran toward us. "Let's eat!" she ordered.

I quickly backed the van into the picnic area. First things first, I grabbed the containers of hot coffee and cider and set them up. Families quickly gathered around, holding the steaming cups with both hands like a lifeline. Meanwhile, I hurriedly put the food on the sleet-covered tables. Determined families fought to hang on to their plates as the blustery wind began to blow sideways.

There was no time to chat as the food needed to be eaten quickly before it froze! Most of the people did not even sit down. They just stood by the tables wrapped in blankets. Some families with small children retreated to their cars to eat. The moment the last person went through the buffet line, the leftover food was quickly loaded into Jodi's vehicle. Nearly everyone pitched in and picked up the area, while Steven and I were throwing the catering supplies into the van. Ready to go, I turned around and hollered goodbye to whoever could hear over the wind and the pounding sleet. Jumping into the van, I rubbed my hands together to try and create some heat. I looked at the clock and was stunned. To my utmost amazement, we had just catered an event—from start to finish—in a record-breaking time of TWENTY-EIGHT MINUTES!

CHAPTER TWENTY-EIGHT

A DAY WITH AIDA

BECAUSE OUR CHURCH WAS A small congregation, it did not take long to meet everyone. One lady stood out immediately. Aida was a petite elderly Filipino woman who dressed sharply. Her presence was always peaceful and calm.

One Sunday I approached Aida while she waited by the front door of the church for her ride home. I introduced myself and was surprised to find she spoke English fairly well, though I had to listen carefully as she had a heavy accent. She smiled tenderly, and then with her soft laugh, she would gently touch my arm. Because we were short in height, I could see directly into her eyes that radiated tenderness. Soon Aida turned and could see that her ride had arrived. Once again, she gently touched my arm and then said goodbye. I leaned against the door frame and watched as she slowly walked down the long sidewalk. I felt myself drawn to her.

Another Sunday our church was having a potluck dinner after the service. Everyone was enjoying the usual homemade casseroles, salads, and desserts. One dish really stood out from the rest. Not knowing what it was, I took a small serving, just in case I did not like it. A short time later, I came back for seconds—and not able to get enough of it, for thirds! I finally asked who brought the dish. From all directions, I heard the name "Aida!" *Of course, I thought, it was "Asian" food.*

I immediately found Aida and asked about it. From that time on, our shared love for cooking and recipes blended us together as friends.

A few weeks later, while visiting with Aida after the service, I asked her where she bought the ingredients for her recipes. She told me about an Asian market nearby. Suddenly excited, she said, "Tomorrow you pick me up and we go there … I show you!"

And so we made plans, though the next day was going to be busy. *I can fit it in*, I thought.

The next morning Aida stood anxiously waiting as I pulled into her driveway. The Asian market was nearby, so I had plenty of time to shop with her before my busy day really went into high gear. At the store, she showed me the different kinds of Asian spices, noodles, and canned goods. Most of the packaging was written in Chinese, so she patiently had to explain what they were used for. This was a fascinating experience, and I could have stayed much longer, but I knew my day was full. We paid for our purchases and headed out the door. Quickly peeking into my bag, I laughed as I hardly knew what I had just bought. Aida too began to laugh while again gently touching my arm.

I was driving out of the parking lot when Aida asked if we could stop at the grocery store as she needed a few things. I looked at my clock, keeping track of the time. We could squeeze it in. I pushed the shopping cart down the aisles as she carefully selected her items. Suddenly, I began to see unusual foods in the cart: tapioca, plantain bananas, and a can of coconut milk. I simply just pushed the cart and enjoyed my time with Aida. A short time later, we got back in the van, and as I drove out of the parking lot, I realized how fast the time went by. I needed to get Aida home.

Suddenly, she turned to me and asked, "What time does your family eat dinner?"

I told her. Then she matter-of-factly asked me about my cooking pans. While keeping my eyes on the road and not making any connections with what Aida was saying, I curiously asked, "Why?"

"Because we need big pan when we cook."

Then it dawned on me: Aida was coming home with me to cook!

Before I knew it, we were in my kitchen, pulling out pots and pans. Aida began to sort through the groceries, setting them aside for each recipe that she had in mind. The first dish she began to prepare was the one I had eaten at the church potluck and loved so much. She called it *pansit*. She wanted to teach me how to make it for my family.

I watched as she sliced the vegetables with expert precision. Forgetting about everything I needed to do that day, I picked up a knife to help her. Everything faded away as I began to savor my time with her. We talked about everyday matters, but I was interested in knowing more about her. So with sensitive respect, I asked about her life. She suddenly stopped slicing and looked up as if to gather her thoughts. Then she began to share her story.

Aida was born in 1928 in the Philippines, the eldest of five children. She grew up in a normal, loving family. During World War II, she was a young teenage girl. The Japanese were invading her country, so there was tremendous turmoil and unrest growing every day. Because of the war, there was no school in session. Her young life was devastated by the conflict.

Not wanting to distract her from her story, I quickly asked what the next step was in the cooking. After showing me, she continued with her story. As Aida continued to talk about her experiences, her voice became strained. She recalled her family running up into the mountains in fear. They were trying to escape from the Japanese soldiers. The sound of trucks coming into town sent people running for their lives. She recalled many times gathering items from the home and putting them into a basket, which was placed on top of her head. Then she would frantically grab her baby sister into her arms and run. Aida feared for the baby's life as the soldiers were known to spear babies with their bayonets. When it came time to run, each of Aida's siblings had a task to do. Her brother was in charge of gathering rice and potatoes to carry up into the mountains. After her family made their escape, they would hide and live under ground in what they called a foxhole. She vividly remembers being afraid when her mother cooked for fear the smoke coming out of the hole would attract the attention of the Japanese patrol planes. They would bomb anything that showed a sign of life.

As I stood in my kitchen watching Aida slowly stir tapioca in a pan, I felt an appreciation for my dear friend. Emotions welled up within me. Aida continued to stir and tell her story as if time had reversed and she was back in the foxhole. I listened intently.

In 1945, as the war came to an end, Aida was able to go back and finish high school. She then furthered her education and became a teacher at the age of nineteen. She soon met a young man who worked for an iron ore company. They were married and had eight children, losing one baby boy to measles. Aida had household helpers, one who cared for the children and one who took care of the house. But she enjoyed doing all the cooking. She recalled her usual recipes of *pansit*, fish head soup, and ginseng mongo. Plantation bananas, jackfruit, and sweet potatoes were cooked into desserts. Rice was eaten once or twice every day.

In 1983, Aida's husband passed away. It was at the time of his death that his sister's family, who lived in the United States, came to the Philippines to attend the funeral. While there, they shared the Bible with Aida and her family. Time had passed, and while missionaries were using her home, she was told again of salvation through Jesus. Then one day Aida asked Jesus into her life. At once, she discarded all the idols in her house. "They are not of God!" she declared.

However, when the church they had been attending found out what they had done, they were expelled from the church. They were hated. In 1992, she moved to the United States to be with her daughter, who had moved here earlier and married.

Just as Aida finished her life story, Ed and Steven came home from a baseball practice. Surprised to see Aida standing in our kitchen, they glanced over at me and then at the stove. Taking in the wonderful aroma, Ed asked, "When do we eat?"

We soon sat down to enjoy the Filipino dish *pansit*—made with chicken, shrimp sauce, and rice noodles—and a dessert called *ginada*—made with tapioca, coconut milk, sweet potatoes, banana, and little hand-rolled balls of sweet rice flour. Aida's handwritten recipe for *pansit* is now laminated and put away for safekeeping so I can treasure it forever.

That evening, after a wonderful meal, it was time to take her home. My time with Aida was an unexpected joy—and all the things that I had planned for that day were forgotten! For what was to be a quick trip to the market became a memory that will be forever in my heart.

CHAPTER TWENTY-NINE

A STORMY NIGHT WITH ROSEMARY

I HAVE ENCOUNTERED TIMES DURING my catering where I faced a problem immediately after arriving at the job, like the time when we arrived at a hall and the main gas line to the ovens was shut off—and I needed to get the chicken in the oven! With no access to turn it on or maintenance man to help us—and two hundred people on their way—anyone who has catered knows panic can set in quickly. When faced with such a situation, time seems to tick away abnormally fast.

Fortunately, I found an old electric fry pan hidden under some towels. Now picture two hundred chicken breasts and one twelve-by-sixteen-inch fry pan! Most caterers can relate to the saying, "What happens in the kitchen stays in the kitchen." In the end, I am happy to report that all the chicken was fully cooked to temperature and tasted delicious.

One night we encountered a problem just as the guests were coming up to the buffet table. I had been hired to cater for a pastor's appreciation dinner. It was a stormy evening as the 220 guests arrived at the church. There were reports of tornado warnings near the area, so everyone was on high alert.

Everything was going as planned in the kitchen, so I stepped out to finish setting the buffet table. Suddenly, the sound of thunder, followed by a loud crack, shook the church. Ed, Steven, and his friend, Becca, went outside to check out the weather. Meanwhile, I went over the menu: Chicken breast with rosemary-butter sauce had been selected as the entrée. Although it is expensive to make, the creamy buttery sauce with fresh rosemary over chicken is a favorite. Some time ago I assured this client that they would be incredibly pleased with the sauce, so they added it to their menu.

I soon motioned for my weather-spotters to come in and help. Then as the storm intensified outside, so did the preparations to get the food on the buffet inside. I asked Ed to fill two stainless steel pitchers with the rosemary-butter sauce. When he finished, he set the filled pitchers in the sink to wipe off the drips on the outside. At the same time, I quickly ordered him to give me a hand. At once, Ed told Steven, who had just walked into the kitchen, to clean up the pitchers that were in the sink. Ed and I carried the pans of chicken to the buffet. Then I walked over to the pastor in charge of the evening and told him the dinner was ready.

As he prayed over the food and asked for protection from the storm, I headed back to the kitchen. Passing by the buffet table, I noticed that the pitchers of rosemary-butter sauce were missing. I quickly ran into the kitchen, ordering that someone get the sauce on as the guests were on their way! Ed turned toward the sink and saw two nicely washed-out stainless steel pitchers sitting there. Holding the pitchers up, he looked straight at Steven.

"Where is the sauce?" he demanded.

With eyes as wide as saucers, Steven stumbled with his words. "You told me to clean the pitchers!"

At that moment, as the thunder pounded outside, so did my heart when I realized what he had done. Seconds passed as the shock wore off. Aware that Steven stood motionless and with a lump in his throat, Becca took his hand.

With no time to spare, Ed scraped what sauce was left in the cooking pot, and I did the only thing I knew I could do—pray!

Now I am not sure if the storm caused the guests to become uneasy, or they failed to realize that something should have gone over the chicken, or the Lord made the four cups of sauce stretch to meet the need. I thought of the loaves and fish that fed thousands. All 220 guests went through the buffet, leaving only a half cup of sauce in the pitcher!

As the guests were eating dinner, their cell phones were ringing. News spread around the room that tornadoes were touching down in nearby towns! A casualty had been reported. The crisis with the rosemary-butter sauce quickly became insignificant with concern focused on the storm outside.

Later, while we were packing up to leave, I went over to Steven and gave him a big hug, thanking him for his great help and hard work. This was a stormy night with rosemary, but it was the look on Steven's face, when he realized what he had done, that I will remember forever.

Steven helping at a catering job

CHAPTER THIRTY

WHAT DOES PIE AND UNEMPLOYMENT HAVE TO DO WITH ANYTHING?

MY HUSBAND, ED, IS A wonderful man, and we have the best marriage in the world! We love to spend time together, even if we are just sitting out on the porch with a cup of coffee watching the birds. One day, however, "togetherness" took on a whole new meaning. Ed was laid off from his job of ten years, and because of a hiring freeze in the industry, he would probably be out of work for some time. Naturally, I became concerned, not only because of lost income, but also because Ed was home all day—every day. One time I thought our time together was going to send me over the edge.

That morning I got up and looked forward to my day off. I had projects around the house that I wanted to accomplish. Soon I found myself skirting around Ed and waiting for him to move out of my way. I wondered if he was intentionally getting in my way. By late morning, he was asking what was for lunch. I looked at the clock and said, "It's still morning!" Couldn't he tell time?

Later the phone rang; it was my sister. We talked for a while, and then I hung up. I turned around, and there stood Ed at my shoulder. He asked, "Who was that?"

Unnerved, I walked out of the room. "Is this what retirement is going to be like?" I snapped.

In time, things changed, and we adjusted. To my surprise, the unexpected happened: Ed started to make pies! Now he had never made a pie in his life, so when he asked me about it, I laughed.

"I'm serious!" he said with determination in his eyes. Almost at once, he dug into my cookbooks.

As you may know, if you have ever made a pie, they can be quite time-consuming and even intimidating. That did not stop him. By Christmas, our son, Mike, gave him a cookbook, *All about Pies*. Our daughter-in-law, Miranda, bought him his very own apron. I told him I approved of his pie-making quest as long as he continued to look for a job. He promised he would. To my surprise, it became obvious that he had a love for making pies—just as his mom did.

After consoling him a few times while trying to master the perfect crust, he had it down. He took pride in his perfect flaky crusts. One time someone dared to ask him, "Where do you buy your crusts?"

They got an intense five-minute lecture on why "he" hand-makes "his" crusts! He concluded they must not know much about pies.

That summer, when the strawberries were ripe for picking, Ed attempted to make a fresh strawberry pie. His mother created her own recipe and was the queen of fresh strawberry pie. Sadly, when the time came for him to draw on her expertise, dementia had set in, and she could not remember even making pies. Eventually, through trial and error, he succeeded.

On another occasion, he decided to make a fresh lemon pie; *fresh* meaning with the rind left on! I tried to discourage him from making this one, but he insisted. Our children were coming over, and he was excited to serve his first lemon pie. Our daughter-in-law was the first to taste it. We all stood near, eyes fixed on her, as she took the first bite. We waited for a response when, suddenly, her eyes glazed over and her fork slowly lowered to her plate. It was obvious— she could not swallow it. Ed burst out laughing, and we followed, wiping tears from our eyes. The look on her face was priceless. At that time, we all agreed that he should never make that pie again!

By fall, Ed had learned to make pies of every kind, and we all had our favorites. His favorite to make was the great American apple pie. One morning Ed hurried me into our car so that we could drive all the way to an apple orchard to buy the freshest apples right off the tree. I thought, *This is going a little overboard!*

But when that fresh apple pie came out of the oven and I tasted the tart, but, yet sweet filling, I thought I had gone to heaven. My parents claimed it was the best apple pie they had eaten in their life—and they were eighty-three years old!

One Sunday for pastor's appreciation, we gave our pastor and his family a list of different kinds of pies. They were to check two for Ed to make. The list came back with every pie checked. The family could not decide on just two!

Now that Ed had accomplished his quest to master making pies and we had all gained ten pounds, it was time that he'd go back to work. He received a phone call from a company he had interviewed with, and they offered him a job.

We do not get to enjoy pie as often as we used to, but every now and then, when Ed asks if we have flour and sugar or wants to take a trip to the apple orchard, a smile radiates from my face. Pies—the fringe benefit of unemployment!

Ed's homemade pies

CHAPTER THIRTY-ONE

GOD'S PERFECT TIMING

TIMING IS EVERYTHING, AND IN the business of catering, it is crucial! From the start of a job to having a meal ready at a set time requested by a client, timing is huge. A great meal ready at the wrong time is failure. A terrible meal at the right time is just as bad. But there are times in our lives when God wants us to stop trying to work things out our way—in *our* time! We can so easily mess up His perfect plan, a plan that *He* has set in motion. We usually do this by taking the initiative, especially when we already know it is not a good idea.

Peace in one's life can be experienced by discovering and accepting God's perfect timing of things. In Ecclesiastes 3:1–8, Solomon, the wisest man in the world, points out and even lists that there are "times" for everything and a season for every activity under heaven.

Unexpectedly one day, God revealed to me in an amazing way His perfect timing.

Our church had its struggles. Frustration was growing as the church was not. We were dead in our faith and in financial crisis. The pastor we had come to know resigned, and the district leadership stepped in at our request. The church was put into redevelopment—in other words, we were starting over.

Our church building had expanded with a wonderful new addition. It sat in a good location as you drove into town, and there was a small body of believers, wanting and faithfully waiting on God's direction. However, in time, much of the congregation grew tired and became discouraged as we waited for "the plan." Soon Ed, who was the worship director, and I were at this point. We felt the need to look for another church to attend—a church that was healthy. This really tugged at our hearts, so we prayed for God's leading.

At the same time, with Ed being unemployed and I feeling the need for a rest, we decided to plan a weekend getaway at a hotel. Because Ed led worship, he made arrangements to be gone. All was set, and we anticipated our weekend away. However, two days before our getaway, we became aware that our outside propane tank was nearly empty. We had no choice but to fill it, costing us plenty! Our budget would not allow us to take our weekend away. With enormous disappointment, I had to cancel our hotel reservations. We had to stay home.

Weeks earlier, Ed had heard about a thriving church in a neighboring town. He felt it would be a church we should visit. So having our Sunday free, he strongly felt compelled to go. But I was looking forward to relaxing with a quiet day at home.

It was Sunday morning as I sat snuggled in my pajamas with a cup of coffee when Ed slowly came downstairs. He was dressed and ready to go visit the church. With a reserved smile, he said, "Barb, I really have a desire to go."

Lowering my cup and purposefully letting out a sigh, I reluctantly went upstairs to dress.

Upon entering the church, we were amazed at how beautiful yet simple it looked. We were greeted with friendly smiles and handshakes. An older gentleman showed us a place to sit as the church was filling up. Then the worship music started up, and Ed quickly leaned forward in his seat, in awe at its sound. It all felt so right.

Soon the senior pastor asked the associate pastor to join him on the platform. They wanted to share with the congregation about a change that was going to take place in their church. Not expecting to sit through a church-business service, Ed and I looked at each other in disappointment. I quickly thought about the quiet, relaxing morning at home that I had given up. It was too late to get up and walk out without feeling conspicuous, so we listened.

With a serious tone to his voice, the pastor said, "For four years, this church has waited for God to give us the opportunity to come alongside or plant another church, but the door of opportunity hasn't opened."

At that point, Ed and I looked at each other, almost annoyed. We were tempted to raise our hands and say, "Hey! We know of a church!"

The pastor continued, pointing his finger upward, and said, "God hasn't opened a door … until now!"

Instantly, for reasons I did not understand, I felt as though something stirred inside me. I looked over at Ed who sat motionless.

The pastor continued, "We have an opportunity to come alongside a church in dire need."

Suddenly, I felt as if everything was pointing at Ed and me, and an overwhelming sense of emotion grabbed me, and I began to shift in my seat. I turned around to see if anyone was looking at me, but they were focused on what the pastor was saying. He explained to the congregation what seemed to be *our church*! Then as if on cue, Ed and I looked at each other. My heart was trying to beat its way out of my chest.

The pastor announced the church and then went on, "We are going to help support them."

It was our church! I sat in awe with tears streaming down my face. Ed laid his face in his hands. Then the pastor announced as he turned to his associate pastor, "And Pastor Bert has prayerfully accepted the call to be their new pastor." Ed looked up in disbelief, and I could hardly keep my composure. "And while I'm announcing this to you, the district superintendent is sharing the news with the other congregation."

I reached over and touched Ed's hand. The service ended with loud applause and words of praise.

The associate pastor stepped down and stood just feet away from us. Ed took my hand and said with a smile, "Well, let's go meet our new pastor!"

Still stunned, we slowly walked over to Pastor Bert to introduce ourselves. His eyes met ours, and with the look we had on our faces, he stood frozen. Trying to stay calm so our words would make sense, we began to share, "We're from that church! We were supposed to be on a weekend getaway, but God orchestrated events so that we would be here this morning instead. We had no idea of His amazing plan!"

Pastor Bert stood looking at us in amazement when he finally said, "Up until this moment, I still wasn't 100 percent sure if I was making the right decision, but God just used you to confirm His plan for me." Miraculously, we stood together, trying to grasp how awesome God's perfect timing was.

For the rest of that day, we were overjoyed and could not wipe the smiles off our faces. We could only imagine God smiling down at us as we sat in the service unprepared for what He was about to do—ready to shower us with His abundant love and grace. It was no coincidence that our propane tank became empty so that He could seat us in that church on that day, at that moment! God wanted to show Ed and me that He heard our heart's cry for our "lost" church and then used us to confirm to Pastor Bert that he was making the right decision.

That winter evening I walked the path that led through the open field of freshly fallen snow and took in the last minutes of a beautiful sunset. I doubled back on the path to walk home with night having stolen away the last of the sunset, leaving the stars twinkling, as if smiling with me. I turned on my iPod, and a song called "Pour Out My Heart" came on, a song of thankfulness to a God who touches us when we cry out to Him. My heart responded. I looked up at the stars, and a deep sense of God's presence filled me. Tears ran down my face.

What happened next, I was never going to tell anyone but keeping it as my own. However, I was encouraged to share it.

As the song of thankfulness touched my very soul, I became aware of God's amazing love for me. Then like in a slow-motion dream, I raised my hands toward heaven. Soon my feet slowly turned me around and around as I moved along the path under the stars as if I were dancing with my Jesus. Then as the music came to an end, I turned my iPod off and stood in place, not paying any attention if anyone was watching. The night was silent, and everything around me was still. The snow-covered field was glistening like millions of jewels under the moonlight. At that moment, once again, I could feel God's amazing love and grace cover me. That night, under God's incredible creation, His love and song touched me deeply.

Many times I've reflected to this event, which is not only a testimony of how God worked in my life but even greater, also to show that God's perfect timing is always the best!

PART THREE

CHAPTER THIRTY-TWO

ROAD CLOSED AHEAD

THE CHARTER SCHOOL THAT I catered for was operating out of modular buildings. The time finally arrived for them to build their first permanent facility. The school director and I negotiated an agreement for me to stay on as their head cook and to use the kitchen as my licensed catering kitchen as well! Although there were going to be some restrictions, I was overjoyed and thankful to have the new arrangement.

That summer, as the school was being built, I moved out of my leased kitchen. That fall, Kris, my kitchen helper and I served our first school lunch out of the new kitchen. Because we needed more help, I hired my daughter, Missy. The year had gotten off to a great start. Unfortunately, that spring, a sad and unexpected situation unfolded, and the school board fired the principal. By the next school year, a new principal was installed. Along with coming all the way from Colorado to Minnesota, came some new ideas, which led to many changes during the school year. Some of them were welcomed, and some were not.

It was around this same time when the desire to write a book about my life really became strong. At one point, I began to write, only to be distracted by the busyness of my life. I tucked it away, knowing it was not the right time.

During my time with the school, it was really a delight to cook for them. I had the joy of watching kindergarten children grow up into third-graders and the fourth-graders graduate from eighth grade and head off to high school. I cared deeply for the students I had gotten to know. Many, I knew by name, and for some, I even knew their family pet's names.

One day my little friend, Julia, came through the lunch line in tears. When I asked what was wrong, she said, "I'm sad because today my parents have to put Hans to sleep."

I knew instantly that Hans was the family dog. I quickly walked around the counter and gave her a hug.

Likewise, during the years with the school, I had formed friendships with the teachers, staff, and Kris, my kitchen helper. I also had the opportunity to work alongside my daughter, Missy. Cooking at the school was my job, but I also had the privilege of sharing my faith and praying for those in need. God had me where He wanted me—but only for a season.

It was the beginning of my fourth year of cooking for the school when the new principal had decided to implement a government-funded school lunch program. Although I had worked hard to manage it during the school year, there were challenges. To better myself at my job, I signed up to take a summer class in preparation for the next year.

The school year had come to an end, and for the last day of classes, I served a school lunch favorite—cheesy bread with marinara sauce and salad. At the end of the day, students smiled and waved goodbye as they passed the kitchen door. You could see the excitement on their faces as they looked forward to their long summer vacation.

School had been out for a couple of days when I stopped back to organize the kitchen for the next year. When I finished, I went to the office to pick up my paycheck. I instantly noticed how quiet the office was when I walked in and assumed it was because there were not any students. I proceeded to walk to the administrator's office. As usual, I began to chat with the assistant. It was immediately obvious that she was uncomfortable, being quick with her words. Wasting no time, she quickly handed me my check while forcing a smile. Suddenly, she looked over my shoulder, so I quickly turned and saw the principal standing in the doorway. Needing to schedule a meeting with him to go over the next school year lunch program, I smiled and said, "Just the person I needed to talk with."

Without a word, he motioned for me to follow him. He asked the administrative assistant to follow as well. We walked down the hall to his office. I assumed he needed to have his calendar. He walked slowly around his desk and sat down. Still standing, I suddenly felt uneasy. Clasping his hands behind his head, he leaned back in his chair.

"You've been loyal to this school for three years," he said.

"Four years," I responded.

He continued as if he did not hear me. "And you've worked hard and done a great job." Then he started to talk faster as he explained his plan to make more changes in the next year.

It was all I could do, to keep quiet, but I could not keep quiet any longer. "Are you trying to tell me that I'm done?"

He nodded.

I suddenly felt like I had been zapped with a Taser. I leaned against the wall behind me. My legs went weak, and I barely heard his words as he talked about next year's contract being filled by a larger food service so that the students would have more choices.

He then added, "You need to remove all your equipment and supplies in the next few weeks as your services are done."

I numbly walked out to my van. Forcing myself to breathe, I turned the key to start the engine. I managed to drive out of the parking lot and down the street before I fell apart. Not being able to see because of the tears, I pulled over to the side of the road. I sat there, devastated. Soon I began to talk with my Heavenly Father, asking for understanding and strength. It put me back together. Suddenly, feeling very tired, I wanted nothing more than to be at home. I needed to tell my family.

That weekend, with the help of my family, I moved out of the school, leaving behind an empty kitchen but taking with me a lifetime of wonderful memories. For the next two weeks, my emotions unraveled and went from shock to anger and on to sadness. Then to my utmost surprise, I was told that the principal resigned and moved back to Colorado!

With no school to cook for and no licensed kitchen to cook from, I felt as if I had come to a sign in the road that read, "ROAD CLOSED AHEAD." I questioned, "Where do I go from here?"

In time, with the support of my church, family, and friends, I began to heal. Believing that God is bigger than all this, I began to sense His hand in it.

School lunch ladies: Kris, Missy and Me

CHAPTER THIRTY-THREE

A NEW DIRECTION

HAVING PLANNED ON TAKING CLASSES in the summer to better my skills in the school lunch program, I had only booked a few catering jobs. But now with no need to attend classes, my schedule was wide open. The unexpected time gave me the opportunity to explore the artistic/creative side of me, so I jumped into a project that would serve a wonderful purpose.

There was a sizeable area of our church's new addition that really lacked focus and purpose. Though it adjoined the kitchen, its stark white walls made the room feel cold and uninviting. The two round wooden tables almost seemed lost in the space. In my mind, the area was a blank slate, waiting for someone to do something. Possibly, it was waiting for me because I had a vision for what to do with it.

Just as God was the designer of the universe, He gives us creative inspiration. I had a vision in my mind of an outdoor café atmosphere—only indoors! So with permission, I rolled up my sleeves and went to work. The area quickly took on a feeling of warmth as the white walls were covered with a rich color of terracotta. Then I spent many days painstakingly sanding, coating, and upholstering thirty 1960s metal chairs with vinyl seats that should have been marked for the dump! The transformation was so incredible that everyone in the church thought they were new. Soon patio tables were purchased, and the newly finished chairs encircled them. I designed and made a café-like awning that hung over the large pass-through window to the kitchen. Refreshments would be served from the counter below. To divide the area into its own space, I set up a wrought-iron gate with an artificial tree on both sides. Greenery hung from patio baskets attached to the walls on either side of the window. It all brought the outdoors inside! Last, a wooden sign was hung above the gate to welcome guests.

After completing the final details, I stood alone, scanning the room around me. It felt warm, peaceful, and inviting. I closed my eyes and asked the Lord to bless the area. I prayed that it would not only be a place for people to go to enjoy a cup of coffee and a doughnut, but also a place to fellowship and study His word. Then I thanked Him for the unexpected time that allowed me to fulfill the vision and how it might impact His church.

Before long, a café ministry grew out of it, and I had the privilege of heading it up. Today members and guests alike have welcomed the many opportunities that have evolved out of this space. It became clear that God had a plan for drawing the people of the church closer together; and He used me to set it in motion.

It was during this same time that our country's economy was devastated, causing hardship for many in our nation and certainly in our community and church. Unemployment skyrocketed with the ripple effect of home foreclosures. Job prospects were slim. When a job was posted, the position was flooded with desperate applicants, grasping for anything. Most had families to support, and college graduates had huge debt looming over them.

Ed, who is a technical support engineer, had been out of work for more than a year. One day, in frustration, he said, "It would take a miracle for me to go back to work in my field!"

Adding to the bad state of the economy, we knew that at fifty-four years old, it would be difficult to find new employment. Because we had already been through the same trial years earlier, we knew the routine of cutting corners and budgeting to make ends meet. We were reminded of the stress and anxieties that unemployment produces. But this time it was different. Our faith in God's provision had grown. We had seen and experienced His hand working in our marriage. We understood that when life's big storms hit, He would see us through. We drew on His strength by turning to Him and thanking Him for what we did have. We persevered because of Him— at work in us.

Meanwhile, just as I had plunged into my passion of designing the café at church, Ed took the opportunity to plunge into his passions as well. This is when his quest to make pies became a reality. But pies were just one thing—for him, music was the other. Ed had played the guitar since he was seven. By this time, he was an accomplished musician, having played in several secular and Christian bands. But it was not until now, with his growing affection for God, that he was compelled to serve in our church's music ministry. He soon became worship director at our church.

Do you see what God has accomplished in and through Ed and me, even during the trial of prolonged unemployment? It would have been easy to wallow in self-pity, fear, or perhaps even anger because "life isn't fair." But God gave us work to do. Trusting that He is well aware of our financial needs and that He will meet them in His way and His timing leaves no room for the emotional and mental garbage that tries to crush us. Trusting Him protects you from it all.

Up to this point, it seems like my life has been like a hilly country road with never-ending ups and downs. All the while I have never allowed myself to slow down. My nature has always been to go, go, go! However, God would soon have me traveling a road that would leave me no option but to *slow* down. To my surprise, in that place, I would delight in the smell of His roses and bask in the light of His Son.

CHAPTER THIRTY-FOUR
COMING TO A STOP

SUMMER WAS WINDING DOWN, AND fall was in the air when Ed and I decided to take a road trip on the motorcycle. The few catering jobs I had booked were done, and Ed needed a break from his job search, which had not yet generated any leads. We were told that riding a motorcycle up Wisconsin's peninsula to Door County was spectacular, and the cherry and apple season was just getting started. So we packed our bags, dressed into our leather gear, and rode out.

For me, there is no better place to relax than to sit on the back of our motorcycle with the wind in my face. I love riding! The rumble of the bike does not interrupt the quiet peace I feel inside. I love traveling the back roads of a rolling countryside, riding along a clear lake, and stopping for ice cream on a warm day. The peaceful solitude allows me to sit back and reminisce, contemplate, dream, and talk with my Heavenly Father. It was during this trip, while taking in the panoramic view of Lake Michigan, that I had a heart-to-heart talk with Him.

"Lord, my heart's been heavy with the uncertainty of my catering business. Because I no longer have a catering kitchen, I don't know what to do."

Lake Michigan seemed to fade in and out of my mind as I continued to pour out my heart to Him.

"I have such a deep desire to write my book, but with Ed being unemployed, I feel I need to work."

With the wind in my face, I could feel a tear being pushed across my face. I began to feel my emotions give way as I whispered, "I want to tell my story." Another tear.

I blinked and wiped my eyes. Looking out onto the lake that glistened like diamonds from the sun, a sailboat came into view. With each wave, it slowly bobbed up and down, mesmerizing me. I wondered whether it was coming in or going out. Then as if a sense of peace enveloped me, and thankfulness poured from my heart, I felt it was time for me to write.

I believe God initiates, causing us to ask—moving us to seek Him. For me, it was not *if* I was going to write my story but *when*. I prayerfully took my request before Him, knowing that He will answer in *His* time— according to *His* will.

It was unclear as to when I would begin my book or how our finances would be met, but it was clear that God's will for my life was for me to tell my story so that others may know just how glorious He is.

Soon after we returned home from our trip, Ed received a phone call from a company that was interested in his resume. This took him by surprise because he had sent out a hundred or so resumes during the last eighteen months and this was the *first* response. Because of months with no interviews, he had been contemplating a career change.

Although he was glad to get a response, he was aware that hundreds of applicants would also be contending for the same position. With reserved excitement, he called back, and a phone interview was scheduled. After the interview, there was a long four-day wait when he unexpectedly received another call for a second interview and then a third! He was told they would respond back to him with a decision within a week. Ed had faith that God would allow this job to be his if it were His will because only God knew where he should work, *but* patience was not one of Ed's strengths— he did not have any! Waiting to hear back from the company was like torture. And I must admit my patience was wearing thin as one week turned into ten days.

One morning, as I stood in front of the patio door, looking out at the chilly morning frost, I shivered in spite of the coffee mug cupped in my hands. The aroma of frying bacon filled the house as Ed prepared breakfast. As I turned to sit down, the phone rang. Caller ID revealed it was the call we had been waiting for! This was it! I picked up the phone and handed it to Ed who suddenly looked paralyzed. I set my cup down, waiting to hear Ed say something. A smile stretched across his face. He got the job! After hanging up the phone, he leaned forward 'til his forehead rested on the wall and said, "Thank you, Jesus!"

Ed was more than ready to go back to work after almost nineteen months of being unemployed. Five weeks into the job, it became clear to him that many things had to have taken place within the company for the job to have been available to him, almost like it had been orchestrated just for him.

In fifty-plus years traveling my life's journey, my speed has always been *fast*! My mother has always said, "Barb started to run at ten months of age and has never stopped!"

My journey has been long and action-packed, but the time had come for the dust around me to settle. I needed refreshing. I desired to drink from the well of the One who carried me when I was tired and torn—Jesus.

I had come to an imaginary sign in the road that said STOP! Without hesitation, I removed myself from my earthly ride. With both feet now touching the ground, I stood and stared into the distance. I caught a glimpse of a sea of roses. I was moving toward them when, suddenly, I felt a tug. I turned. Worldly expectation and human reasoning beckoned me to come back. Tired, I persevered and once again turned to face the roses and continued to walk. Reaching them, I fell to my knees and closed my eyes. I was lost in the scent of roses, realizing that my Lord had brought me to this place.

CHAPTER THIRTY-FIVE

BREAKING POINT

BECAUSE OF THE OVERWHELMING SENSE of relief that Ed had gotten his new job, we were celebrating with praise and thankfulness. Also because of God's perfect timing with giving it, I could now stop to smell the roses and start writing.

After moving a comfortable chair next to a window in the living room, I arranged all the writing supplies, books, journals (I kept a journal of my life every day for fifteen years) to my side. I was ready to dig into my life's journey. Not surprisingly, two weeks into writing, my natural tendency to "go, go, go" got in the way. But God wholeheartedly brought me to a breaking point—literally!

The doors to my school cooking and catering business had slammed shut. Unlike before, when my phone would ring every day from clients inquiring about my catering, I hadn't received one call for three weeks. I even checked my phone numerous times, thinking the ringer was turned off. Then one day it occurred to me the areas of my life had become noticeably quiet as if God had disconnected the constant distractions clambering for my attention. God had given me my dream of an opportunity to write, and yet I found myself wanting to go back to what I was used to.

One day the phone rang, and a friend of mine from church asked if I would cater her daughter's upcoming wedding reception. She was in a bind because of another caterer having a conflict with the date, and she wanted to offer me the business. I agreed to take the job, which was just weeks away. I would have to prepare the meal out of my kitchen at home, which was not impossible, but certainly would be challenging.

Two days before their big event, it snowed heavily. As I busied myself preparing food, my son, Steven, went to work, shoveling snow. He removed an icy mat that was outside the door and threw it into the garage. Moments later, while hurrying through the garage, I stepped on the mat, and instantly, my feet flew out from under me! I crashed hard onto the concrete floor! I immediately grabbed my arm, thinking it was broken because of the intense pain. So off to the hospital we went, and sure enough, it was broken. What a turn of events! The wedding still had to be catered, so my catering friend, Kathy, came to my rescue.

The accident had been divine intervention. It was finally crystal clear to me I was to stop trying to hang on to my old life and use the opportunity that God had given me to write! I was to move forward with the book that He had laid on my heart. So with the approval of the doctor, the nurse formed the cast around my arm and made a perfect space to hold a pencil! As the winter months unfolded, so did my book *Catering for My King*.

CHAPTER THIRTY-SIX

A SINGLE POPPED CORN

IN THE INTRODUCTION OF MY book, I talked about my fascination with God's creative design of food—the very fruits, vegetables, and grains that we eat. The amazing detail of their design is crazy.

Recently, while enjoying a bowl of popcorn, which is one of my favorite foods, I held a single popped kernel to observe its white starchy mass. I thought about how it could burst from a small hard seed of corn. Incredible! While turning it over in my hand, I considered its taste and nutritional value, without the added salt and butter, of course, and the wonderful pleasure it brought. To me, there is nothing better than a good movie and a big bowl of warm popcorn! But I must go back to the Creator of all vegetation—God Himself.

In the beginning, God created the heavens, the earth, and everything in it. The book of Genesis tells us that God first created light and then sky, which held water. Then He said, "Let the land produce vegetation: plants bearing seed according to their kinds."

Then an extraordinary event took place, when God created man. But why man? Couldn't He have had everything just for Himself? So I dug deeper into His word and discovered that we exist only because God willed that we exist. The purpose of our life is greater than our own fulfillment and happiness. It is far greater than our career, our dreams or ambitions.

It is even greater than our family. *We were made by God and for God.* Until we understand that, life will never make sense. And when we look at the glaring inequities of life and its joys and suffering, it is still hard to understand. But God created human beings to know Him, love Him, and worship Him. And because He created us for Himself, His love for us goes beyond our comprehension.

Looking again at the popcorn in my hand, it got me thinking. The fact that a popped corn, which burst out of a single kernel, which came from an ear of corn, which came from an entire field of corn, making it one among billions of kernels; that one kernel had significance! At one time, I felt like that single kernel of corn. I thought, *Who am I among billions of people in the world that God would know or even care that I exist?*

Yet He knew me before I was even born. I am here because God willed me to be here, just as you are here because He willed for you to be here.

To discover "who" you are—your origin, your identity, your meaning and significance—you must go to God because He already knows everything about you! Psalm 139:1–4 says, "O Lord, you have searched me, and you know me. You know when I sit and when I rise; You perceive my thoughts from afar. You discern my going out and my lying down; you are familiar with all my ways. Before a word is on my tongue you know it completely, O Lord."

God knows you completely! Therefore, every other path to find who you are leads nowhere!

So just like a single kernel of popcorn, our single, solitary life among billions of people in the world was made by God and for God, for His glory!

CHAPTER THIRTY-SEVEN

OUR LIFE IN HIS WORLD

THROUGHOUT MY YEARS OF CATERING, I have done many outdoor picnics; but I still smile when I think of the wedding reception-picnic I catered at a park one summer day.

After arriving at the park to set up, I quickly noticed a squirrel nearby. I smiled as he sat curiously, watching me unload my van. Although he stood his ground and did not move, he seemed friendly. I continued to unpack, thinking he would go on his merry way as soon as the guests began to arrive. But the squirrel had other plans!

While setting up the banquet tables, I noticed that the squirrel was inching its way closer to the pavilion. Crawling in a sideways motion, it became clear that both of his back legs had been broken. I felt sorry for the little guy and decided not to chase him away. Soon, as the guests began to arrive, they too took note of the friendly squirrel. While keeping an eye on him so that he did not create any problems, I noticed how quickly he made his presence known. As unbelievable as it may sound, he went around visiting and enjoying the people around him.

At one point during the reception, I did not see him anymore and figured he had had enough of the noisy humans and left. But to my surprise, I found him lying underneath a guest's chair as if he were listening to the conversation. Before long, many guests seemed to accept and take delight in him, but a few did not.

Lunch had been served and enjoyed, and I was cleaning up when I decided once again to check on my furry friend. But he was nowhere to be found. Not wanting to look obsessed, I inconspicuously walked around, looking for him, as I picked up dirty plates and plastic ware. Sure enough, I found him lying under another chair, enjoying a different group of people! The squirrel never left the park all day. Then it occurred to me that we were the visitors in his world! It was *his* park!

Later that day, as I drove home from the job, I thought about how we also are like visitors in God's big world. Because God has always been— without beginning or end—our time here on earth is only a blink of an eye in His time. And just like the squirrel who made himself known and was not going anywhere, God made Himself known to all humanity through Jesus and is everlasting. But unlike the squirrel, accepted by many and rejected by a few, Jesus is accepted and received by a few but has been rejected and even hated by many throughout the ages. The gospel of John tells of people's hatred toward Jesus and those who follow Him, and we see that today. None of this is a surprise to God the Father.

For me, as a young girl, even though my parents never talked about God, I felt that He was real and "something" special. Then in my walk as a Christian, attending and serving in church and going to Bible studies, I have lived my life *hoping* that I was doing what was "right." However, during the past several years, the reality of the cross and its message to the world truly hit home in my heart. Jesus died on the cross to take the punishment for *my* sin. By that selfless act, I became righteous, right standing, before God. I cannot do *anything* to make myself right with God! When I received Christ into my life many years ago, I understood that Jesus died for my sin, but now I believe and claim that to be true. What Christ did on the cross was for my salvation and for my sanctification. He opened my eyes, renewed my mind, and filled my heart with Himself. And like the squirrel who made the park his home and is going nowhere, God has made Himself known to me and has me for eternity.

God brought me to a point in my life where I had the desire to stop and smell the roses. I began to dig deep into the word of God. At the same time, our pastor spoke fervently to our church family about the importance of staying in God's word. His teaching is based solely on the good news of Jesus Christ, presented throughout the entire Bible, and His life and ministry showcased in the four gospels of Mathew, Mark, Luke, and John. Let me encourage you—even challenge you—read for yourself John 1:1–18, where John tells us of Jesus Christs deity (His supreme being) that shows Jesus as fully human and fully God. Although Jesus took upon Himself full humanity and lived as a man, He never ceased to be God who has always existed, who is the Creator and Sustainer of all things, and the source of all life. "In the beginning was the Word and the Word was with God, and the Word was God. He was with God in the beginning" (Jn 1:1–2). Jesus is the word, and God saves people through His word. He is also the light.

God sent Jesus into a dark broken world that is full of sin to be "*the* light" among men. Notice I did not say "a light," but "*the* light." Jesus is set apart from every other light. There are many belief systems out there claiming to be the light that confuse and blind non-Christians and Christians alike. In years past, I too was confused by the many religions and practices in our society and around the world. But Jesus Christ is the Creator of life, and His life brings light to mankind. If not for this light, our sinful nature would never be exposed, and we would live in continual sin. Jesus said, "I am the light of the world. Whoever follows me will never walk in darkness but will have the light of life" (Jn 8:12).

So what sets Christians apart from everything else? Christ and Him crucified! Christianity focuses on Christ's saving work, by means of the cross, at God's direction that we may be reconciled to God, pointing us toward heaven for eternity. Other religions focus on tradition or human effort to try and get to God. The truth is we cannot pave our way to God by doing what society thinks of as "good deeds" nor by doing "religious things." In the Old Testament, people did not approach God directly. A priest acted as a mediator between God and sinful man. Because of Christ's victory on the cross, we can now come into God's presence directly. Jesus said, "I am the Way, the Truth and the Life; no one comes to the Father except through me" (Jn 14:6).

With today's wide market of diet pills claiming and promising big results come disappointment, frustration, and hopelessness. But eating good food in beneficial amounts and making healthy choices are a guarantee for success. Likewise, many religions claim and promise answers to life's questions, but offer misguided half-truths or outright deception, resulting in disappointment and hopelessness. But the promises and claims of the gospel of Jesus Christ, recorded in God's word, are guaranteed, giving lasting hope.

"See to it that no one takes you captive through hollow and deceptive philosophy, which depends on human tradition and the basic principles of the world rather than on Christ" (Col 2:8).

To recognize false teaching, you must know God's word. The only way to know it is to spend time reading and studying, asking God to show you that which is true. In doing so, you will keep your eyes on Jesus.

There are many questions to the mystery of God, and one question that is often asked is "If our God is so mighty, why does our world seem so broken? Where is God in all this turmoil?"

Remember, He has gone nowhere! He is here in the center of it all. God created people with free will, desires and choices, and gave us opportunities to enjoy freedom. However, because man fell into sin, causing him to turn from God, disobedience and unruliness carved its way into humanity, resulting in a broken world. But in the midst of its brokenness, God, who is full of mercy and grace, promised to never leave us or abandon us. As a matter of fact, He sent Jesus into the world to save us, and now He stands at the door of our hearts and knocks. "Here I am! I stand at the door and knock. If anyone hears my voice and opens the door, I will come in and eat with him and he with me" (Rev 3:20).

The will of God is that we seek Jesus and follow Him. The safest place to be in this broken world is in the center of God's will. Why? Because God is sovereign. He knows everything that is going on in this world. He is in control of ALL things! And because of this, He knows what is best for us each and every day of our lives. Left by itself, that statement could make someone upset or angry, especially if life has been horrific. It may be hard to grasp and believe that pain, trouble, and tragedy is considered "best" for our lives; but we cannot see the end of our life's journey, who we are becoming and the purpose of what we have been through. He can. He holds us, our future and our eternity. I know people who have lived through unimaginable pain and suffering. For some, the purpose has become evident, while for others, it is still a mystery. But we do live in a broken world, and it will continue to be broken. Our lives will continue to be assaulted by problems and challenges. When we surrender our lives to

Jesus, He redeems us, all of us, and every part of our lives. "And we know that in all things God works for the good of those who love him, who have been called according to his purpose" (Rom 8:28).

Couldn't God just fix the world's problems and make everything right? Yes, of course, after all, He is God. But He knows humanity's sinful nature—trying to do things "*our*" way—that we will always make a mess of this world, continually causing problems. The good news is this: We can take courage in spite of the inevitable problems and struggles in this life. We are not alone in it. Remember, the ultimate victory has already been won by Jesus's death and resurrection. We can stand in the peace of Christ even in troublesome times! Jesus said, "I have told you these things, so that in me you may have peace. In this world you will have trouble. But take heart! I have overcome the world" (Jn 16:33).

In my walk as a Christian, I have learned that when I give my problems to God, my load immediately becomes lighter. The circumstances may not have changed, but God and I carry my problems together. He then assumes responsibility for how the circumstances turn out. Most of the time they are out of my ability to control anyway. I just need to trust Him with them.

I have also learned to embrace the problems, trials, and burdens from my past as well as those in the present because God is able to use them for His purpose. His purpose is always to bring me closer to Him. When I look back at all the storms of adversity in my life, I realize how they formed me to be who I am today. In the past, God allowed me to "touch the flame"—things that often tempted me—to teach me that I would get hurt or face regret later. In the past, God also allowed me to endure low self-esteem so that I could receive His unconditional love with gratefulness. God also allowed me to carry a heavy burden in my heart—my brother's death— so that in time I would embrace Jesus as my healer. It was allowed that I would face shame and anger from the sexual assault at the cabin to show me that I live in a world of sin and that I could experience the power of forgiveness toward others.

God allows storms in our lives. They teach and strengthen us. We do not grow when the weather is calm but when the storm hits full force. Though at times it feels like we are being crushed, we are growing and becoming stronger.

There is another reason why God wouldn't just "fix" everything. Our self-centered human nature would respond with, "Who needs God when everything in my life is simply fine? I can rely on my own understanding of things."

For almost all of us, we would not need God or even have the desire to seek Him. With this in mind, remember that God created man for Himself—for His glory. In that, He desires for us to have a love relationship with Him—forever!

CHAPTER THIRTY-EIGHT

BACK TO MY BROKEN HEART

"WHAT DO YOU DO WITH all your catering leftovers?" was a question I would often get asked. My answer was simply, "I give away as much as I can because I hate throwing anything away."

After coming home from a three-day pastors' convention, I pulled into the driveway and just sat in my car, exhausted. I did not attend the convention, I catered it! I served breakfast, lunch, and dinner to three hundred people for three days! My feet hurt so badly that when I got out, I could barely walk. Going to the back of the car, I opened the hatch. There, I stood and stared at the large hotbox in front of me. Inside were four full-size chafer pans of chicken bake! With the little energy I had left, I pulled out the first pan and quickly set out to do what I usually did with leftovers. I went to my neighbor's house and knocked on the door. Mrs. Schindler opened it, and a smile beamed across her face.

As she took the pan from me, she said with relief, "I've been trying to figure out what to fix my family for supper! Problem solved."

Back to the hotbox, I pulled out another pan. I continued down the street until I found takers for the other three pans. They were equally accepting of my gift.

I have been known to walk the neighborhood carrying containers or Ziplock bags of fruit, desserts, sandwiches, or whatever was left over from a job. One time, after a church service, I invited anyone who could come to our house for a "leftover buffet." A third of the small congregation showed up! We enjoyed great fellowship, and I got rid of all my leftovers. My family has also reaped the benefit of having a catering mom. We have spent many Sunday afternoons gathered around the kitchen table sharing stories and enjoying leftovers.

When I walked the neighborhood offering leftovers, it was no sacrifice for me because the food was already prepared, and I needed to get rid of it. But how much more special would it have been if I had walked the neighborhood offering whole chicken dinners? Roasted chicken, potatoes, corn on the cob, homemade biscuits, and fresh apple pie—could you feel the love if I came to your door?

God's desire for His people is to please, honor, and worship Him, not with what is left over because we are too tired, too busy, or too stressed; but to make much of Him; in other words, to honor and please Him with "the full-meal deal" or give Him our all.

The more time that I spend reading and studying His word, the more I grasp His absolute glory and majesty, His sacrificial grace and mercy, His never-ending love for you and me, and His mighty power to save. But along with growing in the knowledge of who He is comes the reality of what I give back to Him that is honoring and pleasing, and sometimes they have only been my "leftovers." I work Him into my schedule—mostly on Sunday mornings. But God desires more—He wants all of me. This may seem a bit selfish and unrealistic of God, but when you get to know the Creator of all things—us, the earth, the stars, the one and a half trillion galaxies, and all that is in them (and that is just all we can see!)—it is not!

So what does "all of me" include? What does that look like? It is me desiring to go to Him every morning and being mindful of Him 'til I close my eyes at night. It is me spending time in His word so that I can, as much as it is humanly possible, understand His ways and His truth, which enriches my relationship with Him. It is me honoring Him with praise and worship because He is the King of kings, Lord of lords, and keeper of my soul. It is me serving Him by serving others and by giving of my time and resources by reaching out to people's needs and showing compassion. It is me loving Him by loving others, even when they do me wrong. Ultimately, it is ridding myself of all selfish desires and ambitions, surrendering to

His will—not just a part of me, when I feel like it or it is convenient, not leftovers, but all of me! Sound overwhelming and impossible? It is not.

I want to go back to my broken heart, but first, what is the heart? What are we really talking about? Besides being a crucial organ that sustains life, it symbolically refers to our emotional, moral, and intellectual nature. It is one's innermost character and feelings. Our hearts can ache when we are in love or when we are hurt and wounded. Our hearts can leap when we are full of joy, yet it can be crushed when we are disappointed. Our hearts can break from sadness, loneliness, and pain. And our hearts are burdened from the painful and damaging situations and circumstances that we endure, especially if we drag them with us, like a massive weight, through the years of our lives. That is what I did. The burden I carried from my brother's death, the shame I hid because of one man's actions, the anger and resentment caused by my dad and others, my low self-esteem and the shattered image I had of myself, calling myself dumb for years—all led to a broken and what I thought was an unworthy heart.

One time, years ago, while at a Bible study, we had our usual time of praying for one another's needs. I was always silent about having my needs prayed for. Later, as we were walking out to our cars to leave, a woman came alongside me.

She asked, "Barb, why is it that you are so willing to pray for all our needs, but I've noticed that you never ask for prayer for yourself—your needs?"

It was a good question, and although I knew the answer, I did not know how to answer her because, deep down, I truly felt unworthy of such prayer.

Although I received Christ into my heart years earlier, there was little room for Him because of all the pain and rubbish crammed into it. Consequently, I felt inadequate and weak compared to other people who stood strong in their faith. However, as I grew in my relationship with Him, I began to understand the healing power of forgiveness and His grace that pardoned all wrongdoing that was in my life. Then one day it became clear: With Christ dwelling in me, there was no longer any room for the baggage in my heart. It had to go! As I began to live in God's will by simple faith, an amazing transformation began to take place in my life. Things became less about me and more about Him. The things that took

171

up residence in my heart for years began to fade away. In time, as I put my faith in Christ and what He did on the cross to save me, I found victory and newness in my life. I began to understand God's amazing grace.

Through the years, I have heard and sung along with the hymn "Amazing Grace," but the words had little meaning to me. Now I can barely get through the song without tears. "Amazing grace, how sweet the sound that saved a wretch like me ..." One day, after listening to the hymn, I opened an old dictionary and turned to the word "wretch." It was defined a miserable person, one who is profoundly unhappy, despicable, a vile person. To my reasoning, this did not describe me—but it is me! Not that I am such a bad person, but because my humanness, my sin nature, is wretched!

To understand our sin nature, the tendency to sin, we need to go back to the fall of Adam and Eve: Before the fall, their nature was controlled by the divine nature. But once the fall took place, then their human nature was controlled entirely by the sin nature. In other words, their very nature became that of disobedience and rebellion; they were ruled by the sin nature continuously. And like Adam, so it is with all who are born thereafter, for every one of us was born with the sin nature. And the result is that the heart becomes tainted with sinful thoughts, sinful desires, sinful attitudes, and all that is opposition to God. Therefore, the sin nature is a corrupting force affecting the heart of every man in a terribly negative way. And so *we are* wretched.

Then I turned once again to my dictionary to the word "grace." It was defined mercy, pardon, and special favor. Grace is a gift from God. Jesus and His work accomplished on the cross was and is the expression of God's grace. All of God's grace comes through simple faith in Jesus, His death for our sins, and His resurrection. We can say also that grace is unmerited favor, God's gift when we deserve a penalty. It is His goodness given to undeserving people. Everything we need to be saved and sanctified, set apart for righteousness, is found in God's grace. This includes victory over sin, our own flesh, the world, and the devil. We do not deserve it, and we cannot work for it. No religious, intellectual, or moral effort can save you because it comes only from God's loving mercy—His amazing grace.

"For it is by grace you have been saved, through faith—and this not of yourselves, it is a gift of God—not by works, so that no one can boast" (Eph 2:8–9).

I realized, for the first time, that this gift was for me! Then something extraordinary began to happen—I fully understood what it means to have the joy of the Lord.

* Joy *

Joy that comes from God is different from the world's joy. The world's joy—happiness—is dependent on circumstances, like a job, money, people, things, or power. But those things most always cause worry, conflict, and tension. They are unpredictable, temporary, and often used to cover up our unhappiness and emptiness, all the while feeding our selfish desires.

During the last year of my dad's life, he slowly grasped the fact that everything he had worked for all his life—his farm, his property, his business, his money, everything that satisfied and made him proud—was gone. One day, while visiting him in the nursing home, he said to me, "I have nothing left, and now I'm stuck with this broken body." He was resentful, and he mourned for everything that was lost.

In the book of Ecclesiastes, King Solomon shows how empty it is to pursue the pleasures that this life has to offer rather than a relationship with an eternal God. And so because my dad had lived his whole life for himself and God had little part of it, he felt no real joy in his life.

People, especially in today's world, desperately are in search of happiness but are shaken by failures, inconveniences, losses, even successes.

The world's joy, happiness, has lifted me many times. It has wrapped itself around me when I get an unexpected hug. It has delighted me while riding on the back of our motorcycle, when my house is squeaky clean, or when I have held a grandchild for the first time. But again, this joy is temporary and unpredictable.

True joy, which comes from the very heart of God, is living in a love relationship with Christ, the source of all-lasting joy. It is gladness and contentedness of our soul, not merely a feeling of happiness. In the book of Philippians, Paul was writing from prison, where joy is expressed in his letter. The secret of his joy was grounded in his relationship with Christ and what Christ did on the cross to save him.

As followers in Christ, we are to be joyful in every circumstance, even when things are going badly, even when we feel like complaining, or even when no one else around us is joyful. It comes with knowing and trusting God the Father. God's joy is unshakeable, lasting, can overcome discouragement, and is dependable. Therefore, you can experience it anywhere, at any time, even at the lowest point of your life. The joy of the Lord has given me mountaintop moments—even during a difficult and trying day.

The Old Testament prophet Habakkuk, who faced hard times, looked to God and prayed, "Though the fig tree does not bud and there are no grapes on the vines, though the olive crop fails and the fields produce no food, though there are no sheep in the pen and no cattle in the stalls, yet I will rejoice in the Lord, I will be joyful in God my Savior" (Hab 3:17–18).

* Peace *

Just as God's joy is different from the world's joy, so is His peace different from the world's peace. The world's peace is found in positive thinking, no conflict, or in good feelings. But just like the world's joy, this too is unpredictable and temporary. World peace is also unrealistic in so many ways. Just look at the conflicts that lead us to war, the divisions in and the health of our government, and how the family unit has deteriorated because of the high rate of divorce and our culture that is changing ever so fast. These are only a few examples of what shatters the world's peace. If we go back into the history of our world, even throughout biblical times, we see there *never has been* true world peace. Because of this, especially in today's world, we are desperately grasping at anything to find any kind of peace and failing constantly.

But there is good news: True peace that comes from the very heart of God comes from faith in God because He alone embodies all the characteristics of peace. It comes with knowing that He is in control of ALL things and trusting that He will do as He said He will do! God's peace is unshakeable, dependable, lasting into eternity, and can overcome our sinful nature because we can see through His eyes the understanding of all things. Therefore, like God's joy, we can experience it anywhere, at any time, even at the lowest point of our life. The peace that fills me today does not come from the world or the things the world offers; it comes from Jesus Christ. It comes from salvation, knowing that I will be with

God for eternity, which gives me hope and peace while living in a world of conflict and unrest.

Peace also comes from His loving forgiveness, which washed my past sins away, the present sins I still deal with, and the future sins that will challenge my faith. The peace I receive from forgiving those who wrong me comes only through Christ. That in itself brought peace with my dad as I have freedom from the things of my past. *I wasn't accountable to him, but to God. Our greatest need is peace with God!*

"And the peace of God, which surpasses all understanding, will guard your hearts and your minds in Christ Jesus" (Php. 4:7).

Grace, joy, and peace are God's gifts of supernatural proportions, and they have forever changed my life. My once-broken heart has now been renewed. Because Christ is central to my innermost being, I cannot possibly give Him "part of me, some of the time—leftovers," but I will delight in giving Him all of me.

CHAPTER THIRTY-NINE

MY RENEWED HEART

ONE DAY, AT A CATERING job, I stood in the reception area deep in thought about all that needed to be done. Suddenly, I heard a loud SNAP! coming from the kitchen. Then as I contemplated my next move, again— SNAP! I tried to ignore it. Now annoyed by the snapping noise, I strained to think about the job ahead. Again—SNAP! I looked up and rolled my eyes with disgust. I knew the source of the annoying sound. With my hands on my hips, I quickly marched into the kitchen. Glaring at my husband, Ed, who was holding a damp twisted towel in his hands, I barked, "Why? Why do you always have to snap a towel when my nerves are on edge?"

Everyone snickered as Ed forced himself to hide his mischievous smile. This was one of those stressful jobs, so in my mind, there was no time to play.

Thankfully, Ed's playful annoyance never gets in the way of my appreciation and love for him. We have been married now for forty years— give or take a year. He is the one who always remembers. Despite some bumps in the road, we have been blessed with a wonderful marriage. Although our parents' marriages were not ideal, their commitment and love brought them through sixty-plus years together.

Love and commitment in a marriage certainly can help weather life's storms, but as in any marriage relationship, there are conditions that must be met. Trust, respect, and faithfulness are of utmost importance. Responsibility of caring for each other, sharing in the household duties,

176

and bringing up children are equally important. Desire to embrace each other's families and bearing with each other's problems and trials are also conditions that need to be met. A loving marriage relationship is the reward of willingness to meet all these conditions.

Invariably, because of our sin nature, we struggle with relationships. So at times we do not "feel the love"; we do not want to share or agree on anything, so we rub each other the wrong way. Sometimes walls are built up with no windows or doors to allow communication. Sadly, trust, respect, and faithfulness are lost, ending many marriages in divorce. Human love relationships are *a lot of work*, especially when conditions must be met.

How refreshing it is that the God of the universe loves us unconditionally! He places no rules, boundaries, or conditions on His love for us. His love for mankind is unshakeable; it never changes and will never cease! However, the desire of His heart is for us to love Him back.

Even though I received Christ as my Savior and God gave hope to my life, I longed for something greater—something real. The problem was I could not grasp or accept his unconditional love. As a child and into adulthood, it was ingrained in me that I had to work hard and prove myself worthy to earn my earthly father's approval. So expectedly, throughout my life, I failed many times in my attempts to earn what I desperately desired.

As a young teenager, I had given my dad a pen set for his birthday. He unwrapped it and then set it aside, saying little to nothing. Later, with obvious disappointment, he asked, "Why would you give me something I do not need? Next time get me something I can use." Another failed attempt!

But if I had done something of worth *and* did not mess it up, then I would have earned his approval! Sadly, I rarely could accomplish that.

In my walk and relationship with God, I discovered that my self-worth was centered on the fact that God loves me. I did not have to work to earn it or meet a list of his expectations. He loves me because of *who He is*! He loves me because of who I am in Christ! God calls me His child! "Yet to all who received Him, to those who believe in His name, He gave the right to become the children of God—children born not of natural descent, nor of human decision or a husband's will, but born of God" (Jn 1:12–13).

This revelation changed the way I saw myself through my Heavenly Father's eyes. He saw me as His child. Grasping that was the turning point for me as I realized I *was of worth*, asking for prayer for myself because God wants to hear from me and know that I am dependent upon Him. Now it is a privilege to be prayed for! God's love is immeasurable, and even though I cannot completely comprehend such a love as this, I have learned to accept and receive it.

One afternoon, while out walking with a friend, I was asked what I believed about God. In response, I began to share about Jesus. My friend politely stopped me and said, "But what about God?" I quickly assured her that I *was* talking about God.

I continued, "Because of God's greatness and love for us, He came to earth *Himself* in the person of Jesus."

As we continued our walk, she listened with interest. At the end of our time together, she thanked me, and we went our own ways. It was while sitting on the front steps, resting, and reflecting to my earlier years of being a Christian that I realized just how much I had grown in the *knowledge* of who Jesus is. However, the prayer that I prayed long ago to receive Christ into my life had become hollow—it lacked joy and growth for so many years. Some may say that I had not taken my decision and prayer seriously. I had taken it seriously. I had desperately needed a Savior and knew it. My hollow faith did not stem from unbelief or lack of seriousness in my conversion but from the things of life I let get in the way, like busyness and struggles. I also believe that I did not know where the focus of my faith was supposed to be placed after my salvation. Because I did not grow in my relationship with Jesus, I did not grow in my faith. I remained a "baby Christian" for a long time.

Being a Christian is so much more than just saying a prayer and then you go to heaven. It is a life that has been awakened by the Spirit and is walking in repentance of their sin. It is believing with all your mind and heart that the Bible is the inspired word of God, holding all truth—even at times when you do not understand it—that pertains to this life and the next and knowing that you are a child of God! *That life* brings truth, power, and purpose in and for Jesus.

In time, no longer a baby Christian, I had matured in my faith and submitted myself to be a believer and follower of Christ. The hollow faith I had was filled with the knowledge of who God is, what Jesus accomplished on the cross and how much I needed him. My reason for living has dramatically changed. The things of the world I once loved and sought after, I now hate, and the things of God I once avoided, I now love. Looking back, I also discovered that it was the storms in life that carried me to the place of real dependency on God; it was that dependence that caused me to grow in my faith.

Finally, I have come to understand what it means to be a true, believing Christian. God changed me from the inside out, and this is something only He could have done through the help of the Holy Spirit. (More on the Holy Spirit later in this chapter.) I am not the same anymore but a new creation in Christ. "Therefore, if anyone is in Christ, he is a new creation; the old is gone, the new has come" (2 Co 5:17).

In another words, out with the old self (the accumulation of all past things, good and bad), and in with the new (a fresh new start, a new life in Christ, a separation from my past errors). Then before long, He showed me what a new creation would look like.

It was a cold winter day, and it felt good to have a fire burning in the fireplace all day. Although I had looked forward to meeting up with a group of longtime girlfriends, that evening I hesitated, leaving my warm and cozy house. Our meeting place was usually at a family-friendly restaurant, but this time we had planned to meet at a well-known bar because of their $2.50 hamburger baskets—which sounded good to me!

Earlier that day, while reading in the book of Colossians, I discovered something enlightening. And although, with this group of friends, we never discuss "religion," I contemplated bringing my Bible so that I could share it with them if I had the opportunity. I decided to bring it along just in case.

As I sat listening to a favorite praise song while waiting for the car to warm up, I thought about how I was to finish the last chapter of this book. I had come to the end, and I was perplexed as to how I was going to write its ending. I prayed that God would show me.

As I drove into the parking lot, I turned the radio off. Suddenly, I felt a wave of uneasiness. I wondered if I was nervous or afraid as I pulled into a parking space. Turning off the engine, I looked at my Bible lying on the seat beside me. I decided to leave it in the car as I grabbed my purse and got out of the car. Another wave of anxiety took me by surprise as I opened the door and went into the bar. At once, I could see my friends smiling and waving at me from the far side of the room, which gave me some distracted relief.

I quickly walked over to them, putting aside what I was feeling. After greetings and hugs, I sat down. Soon the waitress came over to take my drink order. I immediately became uncomfortable, and I could feel myself getting flushed. Water was ordered before I could even think. Then a strange awkward feeling came over me as I looked around at everyone else's drinks.

What is going on with me? I wondered.

Suddenly, someone from another table blurted out, desecrating the name of Jesus Christ. My heart was instantly grieved by the slandering of His name. Far from being relaxed, I sat trying to fit into a conversation, when, all at once, my attention was drawn to a man so drunk that he fell off his bar stool. I knew him from my past and had heard that he went through a divorce. Watching him made my heart break, but why? I had seen intoxicated people throughout the years, I thought as he pulled himself back onto his stool. It was only Tuesday night—not a weekend when you would expect to see such behavior. A feeling of sadness overcame me. I wondered how often he sat in that same spot and got drunk.

My attention was drawn back to our table as more drinks were being ordered. Moments later, other acquaintances of my friends came into the bar and joined us. The bar seemed loud, and the conversation became offensive and dark. Soon laughter burst out in response to a story that was told of a dad so drunk that his children had to pull him into his bedroom when he got home and passed out. They had left him on the floor to sleep it off. Sickened by the story, I looked down at my half-eaten hamburger—which did not seem like such a good deal anymore. When I looked up, the room, filled with loud music, seemed to grow even smaller and darker than before. Unconsciously, I had already put my jacket and purse on my lap.

Over the years, I have faced so many crazy, dangerous, and even life-threatening situations that I had become rather tough-skinned. But on this night, something was different. Scanning the bar filled with people, I felt isolated. Even though I was in the company of my caring girlfriends, I wanted to be home with Ed. Anxiety grew as I sat listening to vulgar sexual jokes told by the newcomers to our table. It seemed that my friends' laughter had become forced. I felt overwhelmed with an unbearable sense of despondency. Before I knew it, my jacket was on, and my purse was in hand. Without giving any reason or apology for my sudden departure, I said good night. I had to go.

I turned and quickly headed for the door, only to find my way blocked by a man with a pool cue, lining up to take a shot. With every second that passed, I waited, overcome with emotions I did not completely understand. Finally, he took his shot. I hurried past him and, in moments, was out the door, headed for my car. After getting in and closing the door, I leaned my head on the steering wheel and let out a big sigh of relief.

Oblivious to the cold, pleading for understanding, I said out loud, "Lord, WHAT JUST HAPPENED?"

Then it was one of those amazing times that the Holy Spirit laid on my heart. He said, "Barb, I wanted to show you your renewed heart. Because you are a new creation in Christ, I allowed you to see through *my* eyes. What you saw and felt, that which broke your heart, is what breaks mine."

Sitting in my car, trying to filter the night's events through what I knew was truth, everything began to make sense to me. I finally started to drive home. That night and the following day, I thought about what the Holy Spirit had shown me. There was no doubt that Jesus revealed to me the new person I am. The things at the bar, which caused me deep emotional distress, were hard to endure because they were not of God. This is how Jesus feels when mankind casts a shadow on His goodness and slanders His name. My faith and sensitivity to God had truly grown.

That night my painful experience turned into a point of fellowship with God's heart. It was the Holy Spirit that moved and taught me what I needed to know. He was there in my heart—relentlessly, passionately there. Jesus's gift, the Holy Spirit, speaks to us, strengthens us, comforts us, leads us, and changes us within and at a very deep level. He becomes our life as we allow Him to live in us.

So what is the Holy Spirit? It is part of the Godhead—God in three persons: The Father, the Son, and the Holy Spirit. The Son came to earth and lived a human life in the person of Jesus Christ. He suffered and died on the cross, taking the punishment for our sins. Jesus was raised from the dead and offers salvation to all people who will receive Him, through spiritual rebirth, being born again. When Jesus ascended into heaven to be with the Father, His spiritual presence left the earth, but He promised to send the Holy Spirit to all who believed in Him so that his spiritual presence would remain not just with people but to dwell within them. Before Jesus left, He promised His disciples that in this way, He would be with them to guide them.

In John 14:16–20, Jesus says: "And I will ask the Father, and He will give you another counselor to be with you forever—the Spirit of truth. The world could not accept him, because it neither sees him nor knows him. But you know him, for he lives with you and will be in you. I will not leave you as orphans; I will come to you. Before long, the world will not see me anymore, but you will see me. Because I live, you also will live. On that day you will realize that I am in my Father, and you are in me, and I am in you."

As it was for the disciples, so it is for us today. The Holy Spirit is our guide, and our source of truth. Not to compel or carry us into truth, but to lead us, that we may follow. To have the Holy Spirit live in you is to have Jesus Himself. This is a promise to all who believe. And because of our sinful nature, God gave us the Holy Spirit to convict us of our sin. When we knowingly or unknowingly do something wrong, He makes known to us of that wrong, and so our conscience convicts us. That is when we sense and feel our wrongdoing and repentance is in order.

The Holy Spirit also empowers us to have victory over sinful things in our lives, e.g., drug and alcohol abuse, sexual immorality, pridefulness, unforgiveness, gossiping. But we need to be able to "let go" of our own power, placing our faith in the One who went to the cross where our sin debt was paid and sin was defeated. This is where the Holy Spirit has the power to work in our lives the way He sees fit. Any effort to "hang on" to the least bit of our own power will only diminish the life of Jesus in us. We must keep letting go, and slowly but surely, the full life of God will occupy us, penetrating every part of our being; and believe me, victory will be yours, and people will take notice! However, when we turn from the cross of Christ and shut God out of our daily lives, the Holy Spirit cannot, and will not operate in us, and therefore, we stray and easily fall into repeated sin.

There is so much more to know about the Heavenly Father, and all that He promises us when we draw near to Him. And we do not have all the answers to all the questions now, but one day, for believers, we will. Someday we will see Christ in person and will be in the very presence of God. But for now, I stay in my faith and find joy in my new life in Christ.

In years past, I would have to ask myself the questions "Am I really saved/born again?" "When I die, am I really going to heaven?" "What evidence is there?" There is no doubt in my mind of my salvation. When I received Christ, my soul was bought and paid for by the shed blood of Jesus on the cross at Calvary. He died to save me from sin and death. My eternal home is with Him. The evidence of my salvation and sanctification is clear—the Spirit of God has made a very evident change in my life and in my thoughts. This is nothing I did on my own, but with God alone!

It has been about forty years since Ed's friend, Tom, who had become "a light for Jesus," simply shared his faith outside a bar and invited us to church. That was the beginning of the journey that has radically changed our lives forever. Ed and I are grateful for Tom's faithfulness, and his love for Jesus. We give thanks to God the Father for our renewed hearts.

Looking back, I can see that life has taken me on a journey through many difficult and trying times. But it has also taken me through many wonderful and beautiful times as well. God has designed and orchestrated the events in my life as only He could do to accomplish his plan and purpose in my life. He never ceases to amaze and surprise me by His wonders.

Recently, God had opened a door of opportunity to meet face-to-face with the boy, now a grown man, who was driving the car when my brother Steve was killed in the accident. Charlie was responsible for his death. Because he lived out of state, I had not seen him for almost twenty years. This was the first time that we talked about the accident.

(You need a little more background information on Charlie. Just two years after the accident that took my brother's life, Charlie dove off a bridge into water that was only a few feet deep, paralyzing him from the waist down and leaving him in a wheelchair for the rest of his life.)

Seeing Charlie, after all these years, I immediately felt a renewed sense of love for him. I reached down and gave him a big hug. We quickly caught up on each of our lives and our families. Remember our families were neighbors. Before long, Charlie started to talk about the night of the accident like it was only yesterday.

Drinking and driving at high speed was the cause of the tragic accident. The car, holding five young people, rolled several times after leaving the road. My brother was the only one thrown from the vehicle and the only one who died. Ironically, he was the only one who had not been drinking. Because of Charlie's tragic lessons about those unmixable ingredients, he often shares his story with people of all ages. I was thankful to hear that something good was coming from this tragedy. Because my parents knew the accident would haunt him for years to come, they never pressed any charges. And indeed, he struggled with guilt, remorse, and regret for an awfully long time.

Charlie continued to share more of the details as we continued to talk. Every so often, he would look up at me from his wheelchair, perhaps to see if he should continue. Because I had longed to hear about that night for so many years, I hung on his every word.

Then I surprised even myself when I asked, "Charlie, can you tell me about my brother's last hour of life? Was he happy, scared? Was anything said?"

At once, he nodded, and a smile came across his face as he recalled the time. "Yes," he said tenderly. "There was a girl he liked, and he finally got to sit with her at a basketball game. He was so excited."

My heart leaped! I could have listened to the story over and over, but we had to say goodbye. Before I could let him go, we talked about forgiveness and how that brings healing to broken minds, hearts, and lives. I made it clear that I had forgiven him—my mother and my brother had as well. A tear rolled down his face, and I wiped it away.

Soaking in the last moments with Charlie, I shared about God's love and Jesus's mercy and grace. I promised to send him the story of my life's journey written in this book and the testimony of the One who came to save us!

Sadly, Charlie passed away just months after this was written.

When we begin to receive God's love and accept that He has a plan for us, then we can begin to understand there are doors He wants to open for us. But we need to live in fellowship with Him; first, by receiving His Son, Jesus, through simple faith and repenting of our sins, then by digging deep into His word, which will help us grow deeper in our relationship with Him.

The things from my past, which caused my heart so much grief, were replaced with all the things that God had promised to those who would draw near to Him. In the book of Matthew, Jesus teaches about asking, seeking, and knocking: "Ask and it will be given to you; seek and you will find; knock and the door will be opened to you. For everyone who asks receives; he who seeks finds; and to him who knocks, the door will be opened" (Mt 7:7). As God pursues you, I pray that you too will pursue Him—with all your heart!

FREE PREVIEW

ONE DAY AT SCHOOL, I sat at my desk, fretting, while waiting for sixth-grade math to be called up. Math class always made me nervous, and I didn't know why, except that I knew I didn't like it. Soon the teacher called the sixth-grade class up to the table in front of the classroom. There were only three of us: Carol, Jimmy, and me. On the blackboard, the teacher assigned a large-digit problem to each of us. Carol and Jimmy proudly gave their answer, getting it right. I sat focusing on the number, which seemed to jump around and mock me. I guessed, and the answer was wrong. Again, I guessed and was wrong. Soon the teacher demanded that I come up to the blackboard.

And as I guessed again, she moved me closer until my nose was touching the board. Suddenly, I could feel myself tremble and quickly was unable to hold back the tears. I could hear snickering and laughing behind me. Slowly, deliberately, I could feel the teacher's hands turning me around to face the class, who were all now silent in their seats.

The teacher said coldly, "This is what happens when you don't do your studies. You turn into a dummy!"

Humiliated, I quickly walked back to my desk, my head hanging and my chest heaving from crying. At that moment, the overwhelming realization hit me—I was not smart. I was dumb. Suddenly, my stomach hurt. It was really my heart, but I did not know it.

Days had passed since the funeral, and I still hadn't cried. One day Mom confronted me with an angry tone. "Why don't you cry?"

I could not tell her about the burden I carried. Besides that, I was terrified of what Dad would say. No, I had to keep this to myself. However, days later, my world changed—it was Christmas, and I wanted my brother back. I broke down and sobbed.

During the next months, our home was filled with grief and silence. There was no discussion about Steve's death, resulting in little or no healing for me. And so guilt crept into my heart, telling my low self-esteem to move over. Thus, "low self-esteem" and "guilt" took up residence in my heart.

In the morning, while Bill was outside, Rick could tell something was wrong. "What's wrong, Barb?" he asked.

I shared with the boys what had happened. Rick gasped. Bill's son, however, just shook his head as if this was no surprise. Within an hour, with hardly any words spoken, we were packed up and heading home. The first chance I got to talk to Rick alone, I begged, "Promise me you will not tell anyone, ever!" He reluctantly agreed.

So "low self-esteem" and "guilt" naturally moved over to make room for "shame." Little did I know that, together, the deadly trio was going to slowly pierce my heart and silently kill my spirit. Ultimately, I became void of any self-worth, which caused me to give up. I soon found myself heading down a road of destruction.

Printed in the United States
by Baker & Taylor Publisher Services